SIX PAINTINGS FROM PAPUNYA

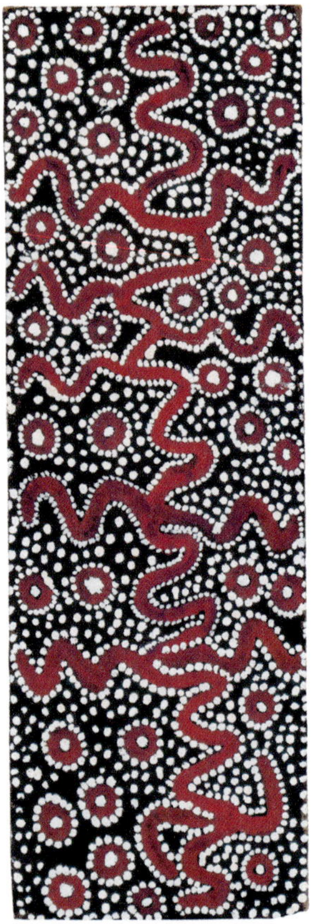

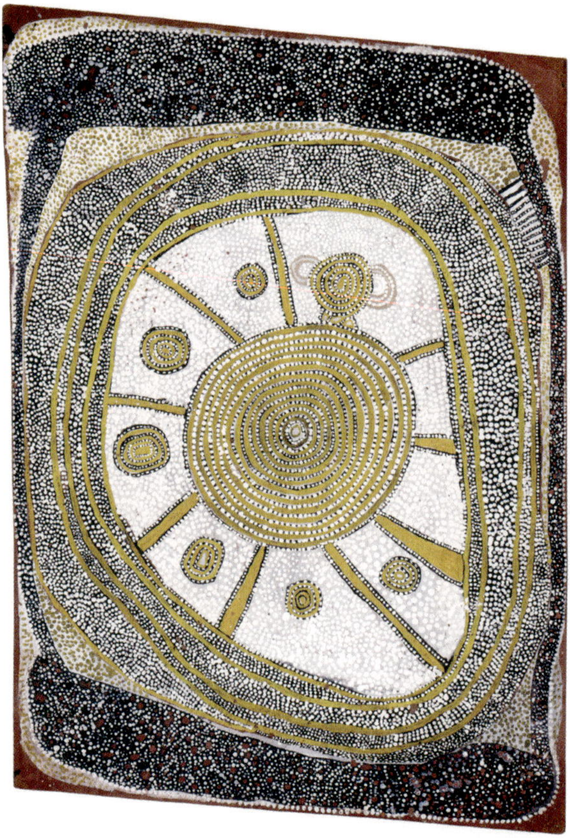

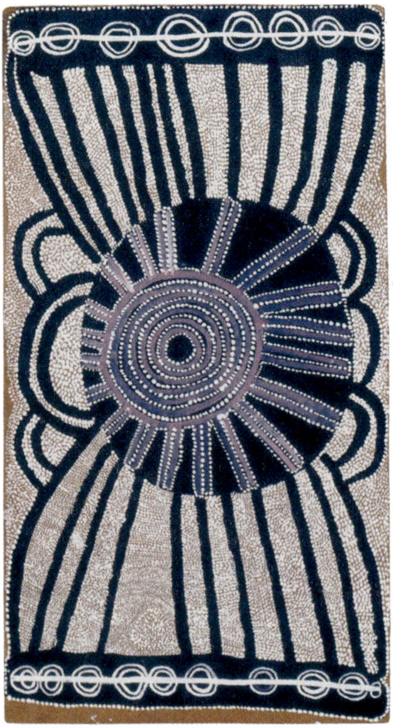

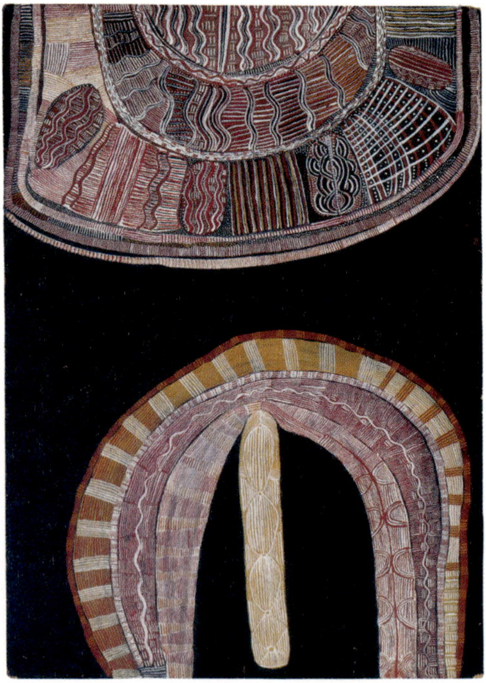

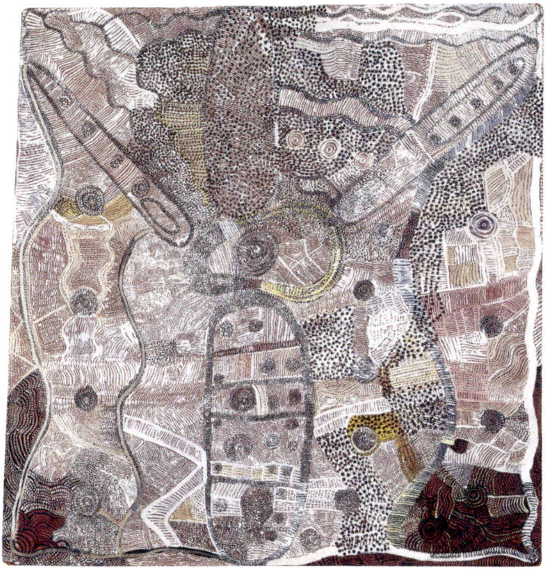

SIX PAINTINGS FROM PAPUNYA

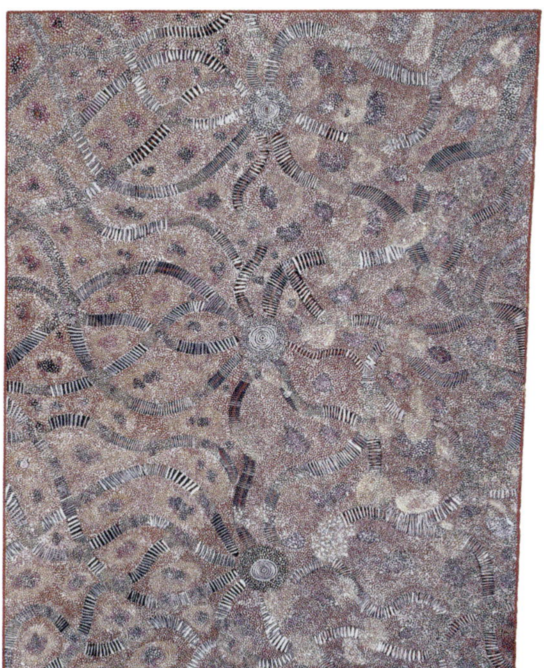

A CONVERSATION

Fred R. Myers
and Terry Smith

WITH A REFLECTION
BY STEPHEN GILCHRIST

Duke University Press
Durham and London 2024

Printed in the United States of America on acid-free paper ∞
Project Editor: Liz Smith
Designed by Aimee C. Harrison
Typeset in Minion Pro, Kalnia, and Helvetica Neue by
Copperline Book Services

Library of Congress Cataloging-in-Publication Data
Names: Myers, Fred R., [date] author. | Smith, Terry (Terry E.), author. |
Gilchrist, Stephen, contributor.
Title: Six paintings from Papunya : a conversation / Fred R. Myers
and Terry Smith ; with a reflection by Stephen Gilchrist.
Description: Durham : Duke University Press, 2024. | Includes
bibliographical references and index.
Identifiers: LCCN 2023056162 (print)
LCCN 2023056163 (ebook)
ISBN 9781478030782 (paperback)
ISBN 9781478026549 (hardcover)
ISBN 9781478059776 (ebook)
Subjects: LCSH: Painting, Aboriginal Australian—Themes, motives. |
Painting, Aboriginal Australian—Australia—Papunya Native
Settlement (N.T.) | Art, Aboriginal Australian—20th century. | Papunya
Tula Artists' Company—History. | BISAC: ART / Australian & Oceanian |
SOCIAL SCIENCE / Ethnic Studies / Australian & Oceanian Studies
Classification: LCC ND1103.P37 M94 2024 (print) |
LCC ND1103.P37 (ebook) | DDC 795.99429/1—dc23/eng/20240511
LC record available at https://lccn.loc.gov/2023056162
LC ebook record available at https://lccn.loc.gov/2023056163

Cover art: Wartuma (Charlie Tarawa/Tjaruru) Tjungurrayi, *The Trial*,
1972. © Estate of the artist licensed by Aboriginal Artists Agency Ltd.

To Joseph Jurra Tjapaltjarri (circa 1952–2022)
and to Samantha Myers (1989–2022)

List of Illustrations ix
Preface and Acknowledgments xi
Introduction 1

1 **THE ETERNAL RECURRENCE OF ORIGINS** 21
Kingsley Tjungurrayi, *Stars, Rain, and Lightning at Night*, 1971

2 **THE CEREMONY IS THE PLACE: THE PAST IS THE PRESENT** 29
Shorty Lungkarta Tjungurrayi, *Classic Pintupi Water Dreaming*, 1972

3 **THE ICY SPIRIT: THE STRUCTURE OF PUNISHMENT** 39
Wartuma (Charlie Tarawa/Tjaruru) Tjungurrayi, *The Trial*, 1972

Contents

4 **INSIDE AND OUTSIDE: A CAVE ALLEGORY** 47

Mick Namarari Tjapaltjarri, *Big Cave Dreaming with Ceremonial Objects*, 1972

5 **STIPPLING PLENITUDE: "THE WATER MAN DOES NOT GET WET— HE IS THE RAIN ITSELF"** 55

Johnny Warangkula Tjupurrula, *Water Dreaming at Kalipinypa*, 1972

6 **DOTTING AND WEAVING** 67

Kaapa Mbitjana Tjampitjinpa (with Tim Leura Tjapaltjarri), *Ngalyipi (A Small Snake)*, 1972

Six Paintings from Papunya: A Reflection Stephen Gilchrist 85
Language and Person Names 91
Glossary 93
Notes 97
Bibliography 109
Index 117

Illustrations

I.1 Charlie Tjapangarti, Kenny Williams Tjampitjinpa, Warlimpirrnga Tjapaltjarri, and Bobby West Tjupurrula making a *Kiwirrkura* ground painting, *Papunya Tula: Genesis and Genius*, at the Art Gallery of New South Wales, Sydney, 2000, 5

I.2 The Men's Painting Room, Papunya, August 1972: Johnny Warangkula Tjupurrula, Timmy Payungka Tjapangarti, Wartuma (Charlie Tarawa/Tjaruru) Tjungurrayi, Mick Namarari Tjapaltjarri, Clifford Possum Tjapaltjarri, Yala Yala Gibbs Tjungurrayi, Shorty Lungkarta Tjungurrayi, unidentified man, and Kaapa Mbitjana Tjampitjinpa, 8

I.3 Unpacking *Icons of the Desert*, Grey Art Gallery, New York, late August 2009, 10

1.1 Kingsley Tjungurrayi, *Stars, Rain, and Lightning at Night*, before May 1971, 20

1.2 Jeffrey James Tjangala performs a Rain Dreaming dance, Yayayi, Northern Territory, 1974, 24

2.1 Shorty Lungkarta Tjungurrayi, *Classic Pintupi Water Dreaming*, August 1972, 28

2.2 Shorty Lungkarta Tjungurrayi, *Children's Water Dreaming (Version 2)*, May–July 1972, 32

3.1 Wartuma (Charlie Tarawa/Tjaruru) Tjungurrayi, *The Trial*, 1972, 38

3.2 Allen Tjapanangka painted for a ceremony, Alumbra Bore, Northern Territory, 1970, 43

3.3 Wartuma (Charlie Tarawa/Tjaruru) Tjungurrayi, *Audience with the Queen*, 1989, 45

4.1 Mick Namarari Tjapaltjarri, *Big Cave Dreaming with Ceremonial Objects*, 1972, 46

5.1 Johnny Warangkula Tjupurrula, *Water Dreaming at Kalipinypa*, August 1972, 54

5.2 The Men's Painting Room, Papunya, August 1972: Yala Yala Gibbs Tjungurrayi, Wartuma (Charlie Tarawa/Tjaruru) Tjungurrayi, Timmy Payungka Tjapangarti, Kaapa Mbitjana Tjampitjinpa, Johnny Warangkula Tjupurrula, and Old Walter Tjampitjinpa, 56

5.3 The Men's Painting Room, Papunya, August 1972: Wartuma (Charlie Tarawa/Tjaruru) Tjungurrayi, Johnny Warangkula Tjupurrula, Timmy Payungka Tjapangarti, Kaapa Mbitjana Tjampitjinpa, and Old Walter Tjampitjinpa, 57

6.1 Kaapa Mbitjana Tjampitjinpa (with Tim Leura Tjapaltjarri), *Ngalyipi (A Small Snake)*, December 1972, 66

6.2 Tim Leura Tjapaltjarri, *Bushfire Spirit Dreaming at Napperby* (formerly *Untitled*), late 1972, 68

6.3 Kaapa Mbitjana Tjampitjinpa, *The Winparrku Serpents*, 1974, 71

6.4 Clifford Possum Tjapaltjarri, *Untitled (Snake Dreaming)*, 1972, 72

6.5 Clifford Possum Tjapaltjarri, *Honey Ant Ceremony*, 1972, 76

6.6 Clifford Possum Tjapaltjarri, *Women's Dreaming about Bush Tucker, Yarlga*, 1972, 80

6.7 Clifford Possum Tjapaltjarri, *Warlugulong*, 1976, 82

Preface and Acknowledgments

OUR CONVERSATION OCCURRED in response to an opportunity, an offering, and a challenge.

The opportunity was afforded by an exhibition in New York of several paintings made during the 1970s by Indigenous artists at Papunya, a remote settlement in Central Australia. Curated by Carolyn Fletcher and shown at the residence of the Australian Consulate-General, *50 Years of Australian Aboriginal Art* vividly demonstrated the early development and the continuing vitality of this art. At the lagging end of COVID-19 pandemic isolation, this extraordinary set of paintings rested quietly on the walls of the residency, open to extended and uninterrupted engagement with them on a beautiful New York afternoon in July 2022. The Papunya paintings, all from the collection of John and Barbara Wilkerson, were accompanied by contemporary works by desert-based artists selected from the collection of Steve Martin and Anne Stringfield. We thank Carolyn Fletcher and John Wilkerson for their warm encouragement of this project.

The artists gathered at Papunya in the early 1970s, when the artist cooperative named Papunya Tula Artists was founded, and offered their paintings to other peoples at Papunya and to the wider world beyond as embodiments of their Dreaming. In proffering this most important gift, they sought responses of a similar kind. We are deeply indebted to the patient contributions of Wartuma Tjungurrayi, Shorty Lungkarta Tjungurrayi, Uta Uta Tjangala, Freddy West Tjakamarra, Yanyatjarri Tjakamarra, and Bobby West Tjupurrula. Papunya Tula Artists Pty. Ltd. has been an inspiration, a support, and literally a home during many phases of research from 1973 through the present. It remains a major ongoing support of Indigenous aspiration and accomplishment. While the artists involved are no longer alive, their paintings continue to invite response.

The challenge is to respond in ways adequate to this invitation, to offer in return something of equivalent value, and to do so to the best of one's particular abilities. In our case—Myers's as an anthropologist and Smith's as an art historian, art critic, and critical theorist, with both of us having decades-long engagement with, in turn, these artists and this art—our responsibility is to open ourselves to these objects, to see as best we can what they have to say, and to say what it is that we are seeing.

We do so while listening to the voices of many others who have previously responded to the same invitation. We also owe much to the work and the collegiality of T. G. H. Strehlow, Nancy Munn, Geoffrey Bardon, R. G. (Dick) Kimber, Eric Michaels, Judith Ryan, Annemarie Brody, J. V. S. Megaw, Peter Sutton, Christopher Anderson, Françoise Dussart, Paul Carter, Hetti Perkins, Vivien Johnson, John Kean, Luke Scholes, Paul Sweeney, Cara Pinchbeck, Marina Strocchi, Philip Jones, Roger Benjamin, Ian McLean, Jennifer Biddle, and Henry Skerritt. For their valuable comments on our work in progress for this project and their responses to questions related to it, we thank Ian McLean, Henry Skerritt, John Kean, Paul Sweeney, Howard Morphy, Françoise Dussart, and Jennifer Biddle.

We especially thank Stephen Gilchrist for his insightful reflections, which have added an important dimension to our efforts.

For their assistance in obtaining and providing permissions and images, we thank the Aboriginal Artists Agency Ltd., Andrea R. Potochniak, Anthony Wallis, the Art Gallery of New South Wales, the Art Gallery of South Australia, the Art Gallery of Western Australia, Clothilde Bullen, D'Lan Contemporary, D'Lan Davidson, Faye Ginsburg, Michael Jensen, Laura Masters, Papunya Tula Artists Pty. Ltd., Terry Parry, Cara Pinchbeck, Grant Rundell, Sue Sauer, Lisa Slade, Muuki Taylor and Nyalangka Taylor, Bobby West Tjupurrula, and Matthew Pinta Tjapangarti.

At Duke University Press, we thank Ken Wissoker for his enthusiastic support; the anonymous reviewers for their constructive comments; and Ryan Kendall and Liz Smith for their expert facilitation of the process.

Royalties will go to the Western Desert Nganampa Walytja Palyantjaku Tjutaku Aboriginal Corporation, in support of their Purple House health service, based in Alice Springs, which has provided medical and cultural support to allow artists and others to return to their country.

INTRODUCTION

> We started it, like a bushfire, this painting business, and it went every way: north, east, south, west, with Papunya in the middle.
> **—Long Jack Phillipus, 2010**

Acrylic paintings by Indigenous peoples from Australia's Western Desert have captivated audiences for more than fifty years. Their arrival has often prompted expressions of surprise that those who were once considered to have the simplest material culture among living humanity could create works that spark such aesthetic resonance. The origin of these works in what seemed to be unfathomable cultural worlds, their evident yet impenetrable sacredness, aroused widespread fascination among secular, disenchanted moderns—not least among modernist artists, critics, curators, and collectors. Such discourses of surprise and discovery have ebbed in recent years as the world becomes more and more aware of the multiplicity of its contemporaneous differences. Yet taste for this art has not subsided, and markets for it continue to grow. In such contexts, how are these paintings to be understood as contemporary artworks?

We propose that this question may be productively answered by close and careful looking at specific paintings, at a selection from among the earliest produced at Papunya in 1971 and 1972, the place and time widely regarded as the origin of the contemporary Aboriginal art moment.

During the decades since then, Aboriginal cultural objects have risen within the hierarchical schema of the Western art-culture system, from being seen as examples of cultural artifacts to achieving the status of singular, "high art" objects, repositories of concentrated aesthetic value and of significant cultural meaning.[1] This transit from the ethnographic museum to the fine art gallery or museum has been much desired by many supporters of Indigenous Australians, fellow artists, and collectors. It has also been celebrated by Indigenous activists and artists as recognition of their aesthetic achievement, releasing their peoples from their subhuman classification among the flora and fauna of natural history and from the living death of representing the "primitive" stages of human evolution.

The artworks under discussion were created at the intersection of Anglo-Australian and Indigenous culture and society, exhibiting a power that calls to many. They were clearly intended to communicate Indigenous values and understandings of the world and the place of humans in that world. They emerged—beautiful and strange—as "gifts" offered to those who had presumed to colonize them.

This book is a conversation between an anthropologist/ethnographer and an art critic, historian, and theorist. We are aware of the historical implication of anthropology within colonial systems of racial classification and in the ongoing persistence of cultural control. Similarly, we recognize that art history's service to cultural privilege and to the demands of art markets can discolor its value as a practice of disinterested research and education. Nevertheless, as we will show, several anthropologists and art historians have contributed significantly through their writings and exhibitions to the scholarly understanding of this art and to its public appreciation.[2]

Our focus or subject is six paintings created by Indigenous men from the "Aboriginal settlement" of Papunya in the early 1970s. These works should be understood as transpositions of their *Tjukurrpa*—the corpus of knowledge of "Country" (or landscape), ancestral beings and stories, traditionally performed in ceremony, with decorated objects and body decoration—onto two-dimensional surfaces using acrylic or polymer paint. In that sense, these objects are an emergent form. At the same time, they are anchored in and express elements of a cultural tradition of great antiquity and profound depth.

The conversation in this volume brings our two disciplines together to do what these paintings ask of us: to respond to their several dimensions in a spirit—and, we hope, a practice—of coevality.

Transcultural Curating

One of the disciplinary practices that anthropologists and art historians have in common is curating. Exhibitions in museums and galleries are the occasions on which the research materials and the interpretive insights of both professions are made public. These are reinforced by publications of many kinds, from specialist journals through scholarly monographs to books intended for the general public. The outpouring of art from the remote communities has called these professions together, among others, and asked them, in effect, to use their expertise to amplify its voice, to use their languages—so well established in the wider world—to help build bridges across which certain kinds of understanding might walk. Each profession has much to offer, but the offerings are different. Whatever their internal differences of approach, anthropologists study the processes of human cultures and the interactions of people and the articulation of these in social formations. Art historians prioritize the creation of works of art, seeking to understand how, when, and why they were made, and with which effects. For fifty years now, outstanding practitioners of these two disciplines have been drawn to study and to write about the art made at Papunya and in its region. Their contributions, however, do not constitute the whole bridge, the entire field of interpretation that enables the transcultural conversation to take place. The artists have also recruited another important modern discipline to assist their cause: curating as a practice of collecting, caring for, and exhibiting works of art.

Today, catalogs of major exhibitions of Indigenous art will typically feature statements by the artists, an essay by the curator about the aims of the exhibition, another by the anthropologist closest to the community, and one by an art historian reflecting on the evolution of the art on show. All have distinct informational and educational purposes, yet the exhibition as a total experience implies that these purposes are convergent. And for exhibitions of Indigenous art, as well as for the discourse around it, the implication is that Indigenous values should be foregrounded. These are defined by Yamatji curator and scholar Stephen Gilchrist as "presencing the ancestral, surfacing alternative histories, spatialising the deep local, and enfolding audiences in evocations of the ceremonial."[3] Such values were strikingly evident in the exhibition *Papunya Tula: Genesis and Genius*, curated by Hetti Perkins in 2000, as they have been, since the 1990s, in the exhibitions and projects of several other Indigenous curators, among them Djon Mundine, Brenda L. Croft, Margo Neale, and Gilchrist himself.[4]

We both have very strong memories of the exhibition *Papunya Tula: Genesis and Genius*, held at the Art Gallery of New South Wales, Sydney, as part of the cultural program of the 2000 Summer Olympics. It was arranged by Arrernte and Kalkadoon curator Hetti Perkins, along with two other Indigenous curators, Cara Pinchbeck and Jonathan Jones.[5] From rooms filled with mostly small, early paintings on boards to large-scale canvases, often collectively painted, many by women artists, and a *Kiwirrkura* ground painting using public symbols from sacred ceremony made by several of the artists, the 150 works were selected in close consultation with the communities to show the origins of art making at the remote desert settlement of Papunya since the early 1970s ("Genesis") and to emphasize the extraordinary quality of its continuing creativity ("Genius") (see fig. I.1). In a recent interview, Perkins tells how she faced down opposition to the use of the word "genius" in the title and how she dealt with the controversy caused by her decision to display the works without titles and wall texts. Instead, she had numbered them and offered sheets in each room with the titles and other basic information:

> Because people walk up and read the title and move on. We really wanted to take that out and make people look at the pictures. Our guiding philosophy was that these artists are making these pictures for a reason: for you to look at them and to feel them and hear them, as well as see them.... [T]hat show really had to cut a line through the dross, the mythologizing of "songlines" and "spirituality" and so on. We wanted to show that these are actually concrete works made by people who have their own histories and stories. They are not just generic stories, but they are their own, as you can see in the work. Because everybody's work is different. That's the part that really materializes in the paintings.... [T]he effect of a good show is, that you see that there are personalities, that there are distinctive engagements, and so on. That's a huge thing for people to recognize.[6]

In the interview, she was responding to the following remark by one of us (Fred Myers) who had explained the value of his research into the paintings, following the invitation to do so by his volume's Pintupi authors, first issued in 1973 and renewed to this day: "The thing is that people don't actually know what's in the painting. And if you know something about what is in the paintings, you can see what they've done, like what makes them artists, right? Of course, it's beautiful, and they have a great sense of color and balance and all of those things, but there is more there."[7] Working out ways to engage those who "walk up and read the title and move on" remains a central challenge

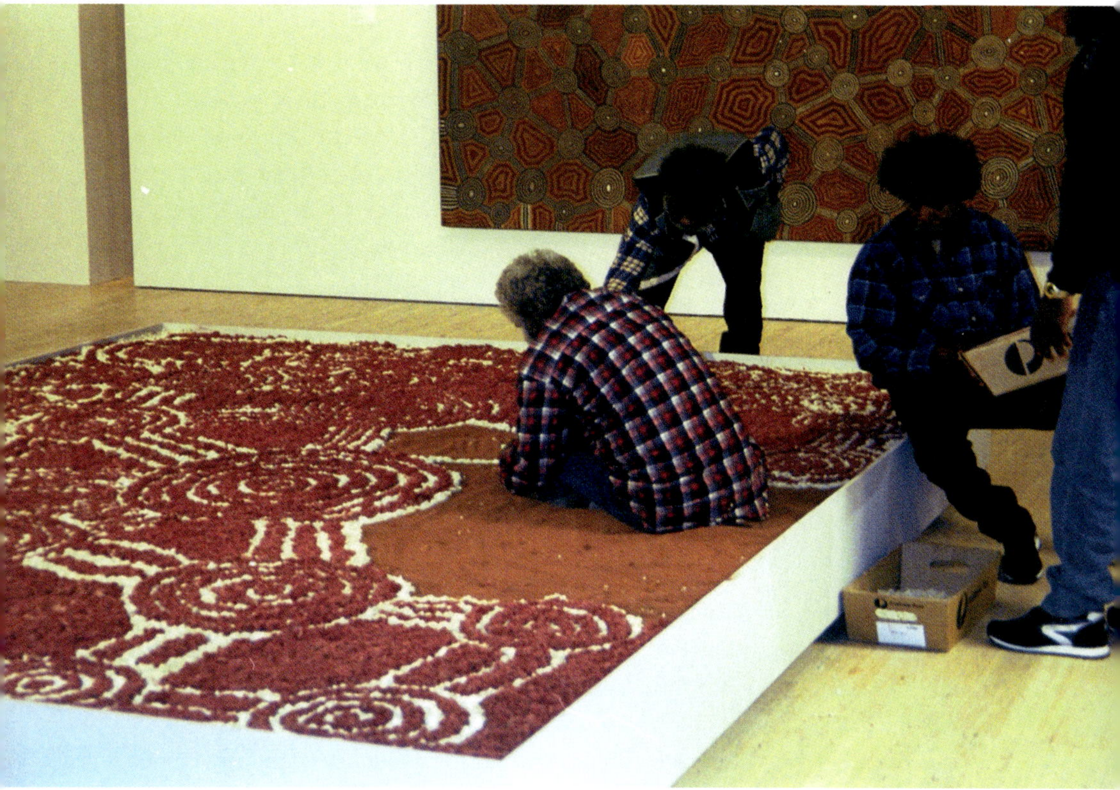

I.1 Charlie Tjapangarti, Kenny Williams Tjampitjinpa, Warlimpirrnga Tjapaltjarri, and Bobby West Tjupurrula making a *Kiwirrkura* ground painting, *Papunya Tula: Genesis and Genius*, at the Art Gallery of New South Wales, Sydney, 2000. Photograph by Fred Myers. Used with permission of participant and living relative Bobby West Tjupurrula.

to all involved in the many-voiced discourse that is contemporary Australian Indigenous art. So is the need to articulate the more that is there: more than the mythologizing "dross"; more than the simple, shorthand "stories" that can too often bring looking to an end, as if that is all there is to see; and more than the "great sense of color and balance" and all those self-isolating aesthetic "things."

Story and Form

With these challenges and examples in mind, we set out to tackle a smaller issue within this larger whole, one that is, nevertheless, at the essence of art writing: the offering of detailed, descriptive interpretations and evaluations of particular works of art. Despite the by now quite large literature about this art, close, extended readings of individual works are relatively rare. We wondered whether something helpful might emerge if we two—longtime but occasional interlocutors, and representatives of two disciplines that have focused on this art—were to seize an opportunity to stand before some works by Australian Indigenous artists and to work together to articulate what these paintings were inviting us to see. In our first exchange about these matters, over twenty years ago, Myers posed the problem in these terms:

> The contemporary traffic in culture in this domain connects not simply the Aboriginal community and the "Western" market, but also distinctive disciplinary traditions with respect to the rather vexed object of "Aboriginal acrylic painting"—an "awkward relationship" between what I would call a "localism" (which I identify with anthropology) and a "cosmopolitanism" (which I identify with what I will loosely call "the art world"), as the objects and activities observed by anthropologists circulate as new forms of difference.[8]

To test where this awkwardness stood now, we took up a chance to look at not just some random sample of "Aboriginal acrylic painting," but a cluster of what were among the earliest painted at Papunya. The proximate occasion of our conversation was an exhibition of several works from the John and Barbara Wilkerson collection, shown at the residence of the Australian Consulate-General in New York. Along with contemporary works by desert-based artists, selected from the collection of Steve Martin and Anne Stringfield, for a few months during 2022, the exhibition made 1 Beekman Place, in Midtown Manhattan overlooking the East River, seem a distant outpost of the remote Indigenous communities in the deserts of Australia.

While our conversation as presented here is an edited and expanded transcript of what was said, it includes several notes aimed at informing those not familiar with the artists, the movement, or the circumstances of its flourishing. In the remainder of this introduction, we will outline these circumstances. We will then sketch out the main stages in the discourse around this art, to introduce some of its themes and many of its protagonists, with whom we engage as we talk about the paintings.

Papunya Tula

Understanding the paintings requires understanding where, when, and what they came from. The township of Papunya was established by the Australian federal government in 1959 around a reliable water source (the bore at Lyappa soakage), 240 kilometers (150 miles) west of Alice Springs. It aimed to serve as a settlement and a place of cultural assimilation for a variety of Indigenous peoples who had, over the preceding half century, been displaced from their traditional homelands by pastoralism, missionaries, drought, and, in the 1950s and 1960s, the policy of securing a complete census of the continent's population. The town sits on the land of the Honey Ant ancestors and their descendants, *tjarla* in the Pintupi-Luritja language of the area. As settlement advanced, the white administrative center was surrounded by the homes of several peoples, the Western Arrernte closest to the middle, as it is their traditional land, and the other peoples—the Anmatyerr, the Warlpiri, the Pintupi, and the Luritja—camping in the directions oriented toward their traditional lands. Papunya also had its own local cultural politics and projects. Although many inhabitants were in frequent contact with non-Indigenous station owners, contract workers, welfare officers, and the like, others were relatively recent arrivals at such settlements. Contacts with other Indigenous peoples had occurred over millennia, yet they required renegotiation in such changing circumstances. The township was designed for 400 people, but by the early 1970s the Indigenous population of Papunya was close to 1,400. Renegotiation was a constant factor in everyday life for everyone at the settlement, including those interested in painting. As we shall see, renegotiation became a definitive aspect of the artistic practice.

One key moment was the painting of five murals on the exterior walls of the Papunya School between June and August 1971. By far the largest symbols displayed on the most prominent wall were devoted to the Honey Ant Dreaming. Up to forty men from several language groups were involved at various times, but Kaapa Mbitjana Tjampitjinpa was the leading Indigenous artist. Accompanied by Mick Wallankarri Tjakamarra, the elder with main authority for the Honey Ant Dreaming at this place, Tjampitjinpa had approached Geoffrey Bardon, a recently arrived, young art teacher, who would become the first advisor, documenter, and proponent of these artists, with a sketch for the main mural. Bardon recalls the moment when he intervened in the painting process to question the inclusion of "European" figurative renderings of honey ants in parts of the design. After consulting the other men present, Kaapa erased these figures and replaced them with publicly permissible versions of signs for the presence of these sacred ancestors. Bardon exults: "It was a moment of glory for Western Desert people as we, Old Bert Tjakamarra, Old Mick Tjakamarra, Bill Stockman Tjapaltjarri and Long Jack Phillipus and the others, watched and the first hieroglyph was put on the wall, lovingly and beautifully with Kaapa's sinuous, marvelous technique."[9] Three years later, these murals, and one by Bardon himself pictur-

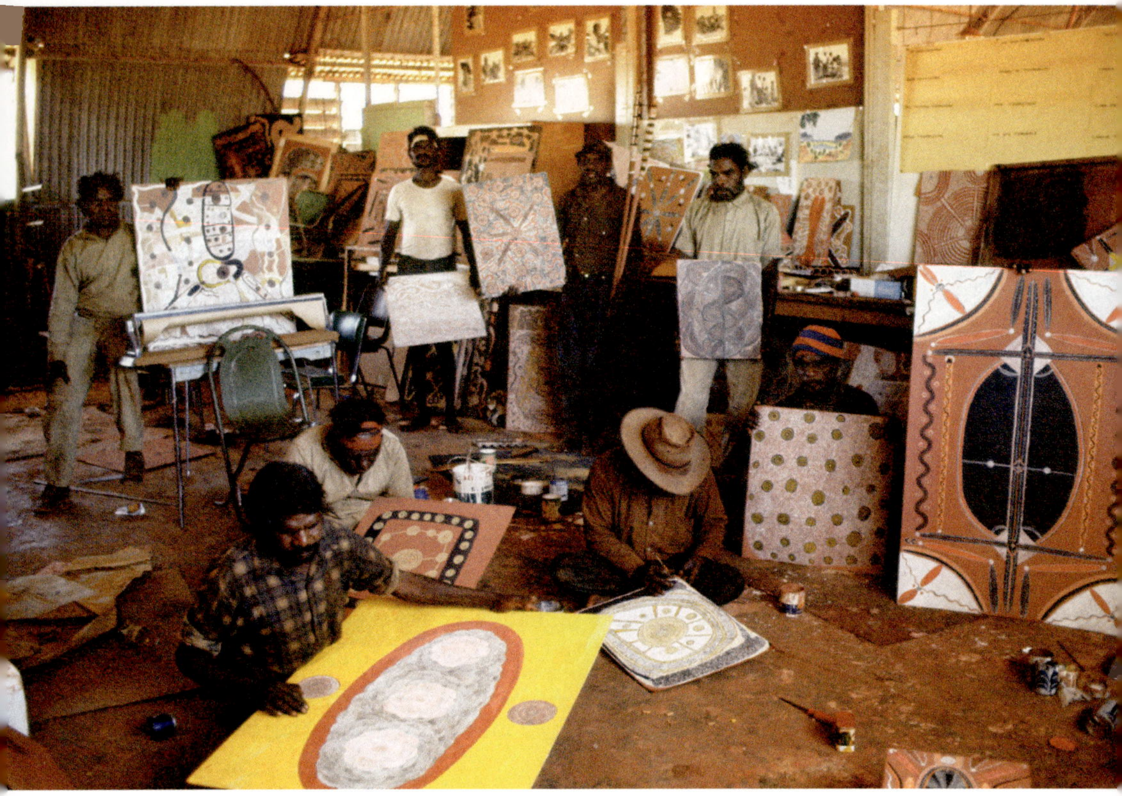

I.2 The Men's Painting Room, Papunya, August 1972. *Back row, from left:* Johnny Warangkula Tjupurrula, Timmy Payungka Tjapangarti, Wartuma (Charlie Tarawa/Tjaruru) Tjungurrayi, Mick Namarari Tjapaltjarri. *Front row, from left:* Clifford Possum Tjapaltjarri, Yala Yala Gibbs Tjungurrayi, Shorty Lungkarta Tjungurrayi, unidentified man, Kaapa Mbitjana Tjampitjinpa (hidden by painting). Photograph by Michael Jensen.

ing the school community in ideal terms, were painted over during a routine renovation of the school.

It is estimated that between 1,200 and 1,500 paintings on boards of various kinds were produced at Papunya between 1971 and 1973. In his 2004 book, *Papunya: A Place Made after the Story*, Bardon documents nearly five hundred of them.[10] A few hundred quickly entered the collection of the Museum and Art Gallery of the Northern Territory, where they were rarely shown due to concerns about their secret content. Many were acquired in Alice Springs as souvenirs. Others entered museums or private collections in Australia and abroad. Despite the assiduous efforts of marketeers, especially since the 1990s, many are presumed lost or destroyed.[11] In August 1972, the Papunya Art and Craft Council was established to manage the distribution of art materials and the sale of works. Four months later, the artists renamed it Papunya Tula, evoking a small hill east of the town, a Honey Ant Dreaming site. In 2022, Papunya Tula Artists Pty. Ltd., the artist cooperative, celebrated fifty years of continuous activity, which shows no signs of diminishing.

The Wilkerson Collection

The John and Barbara Wilkerson collection was put together mostly in the mid-1990s and the early 2000s, when several early works by the painters who became Papunya Tula Artists Pty. Ltd. came onto the secondary market (that is, paintings that had been produced and sold earlier were being reentered for sale by the owners). This was developing as a new market, establishing fresh value in these works as "important Aboriginal art." Tim Klingender, Sotheby's auctioneer, was its primary champion. The stirring of this market was met with newspaper coverage that drove local and international recognition that a significant artistic phenomenon had emerged. The Wilkerson collection was formed in this context. It was inspired by an encounter in the early 1990s with a Water Dreaming painting by Johnny Warangkula Tjupurrula, the only Papunya board shown at the Museum and Art Gallery of the Northern Territory in Darwin for many decades. Fittingly, a collection highlight is Warangkula's acclaimed *Water Dreaming at Kalipinypa*, painted in 1972, which set price records. We discuss it in the conversation that follows. Most scholars and aficionados regard the Wilkerson collection as including some of the jewels of the early periods of the painting movement at Papunya and as certainly the best collection of such work outside of Australia. Several paintings from the collection have been loaned and exhibited at various venues around the world in accordance with the Wilkersons' aim to promote the "connoisseurship, scholarship, and education" through the sharing of their collection.[12]

Some fifty "early Aboriginal paintings from Papunya," all from the Wilkerson collection, were presented in the exhibition *Icons of the Desert*, which was shown at the Herbert Johnson Museum, Cornell University, Ithaca, New York, from January 10 to April 5, 2009; then at the Fowler Museum at the University of California, Los Angeles, from May 3 to August 2, 2009; and ending its tour at the Grey Art Gallery at New York University, New York City, from September 1 to December 5, 2009 (see fig. I.3). It was guest curated by the Australian art historian Roger Benjamin with help from Andrew Weislogel, an associate curator at the originating institution. The overall framework was articulated by Benjamin in an essay in the exhibition catalog, identifying what he presented as the birth of an international art movement: "Beauty has many forms, but it is not every day that a new kind of beauty is born to the world."[13] The installations differed at the separate sites, with the Grey Art Gallery deciding to place some paintings that the descendants of the painters regarded as not for public display in a more secluded gallery, a procedure replicated to some extent in the catalog, which removed several images of paintings from the printed catalog and placed them in a separate insert that would not travel to Australia.[14] Painters from Papunya Tula or their descendants were present at two of these venues. Various accompanying educational programs were offered. Myers, who had an ongoing relationship with painters from Papunya Tula since the early 1970s, participated in the catalog production and in events at the Grey Art Gallery and the Herbert Johnson Museum.

I.3 Unpacking *Icons of the Desert*, Grey Art Gallery, New York, late August 2009. Fred Myers looking at Shorty Lungkarta Tjungurrayi, *Classic Pintupi Water Dreaming*, 1972. *Children's Water Dreaming (Version 2)*, 1972, is at left. Kingsley Tjungurrayi's *Stars, Rain, and Lightning at Night*, 1971, is in the background. Photograph by Faye Ginsburg.

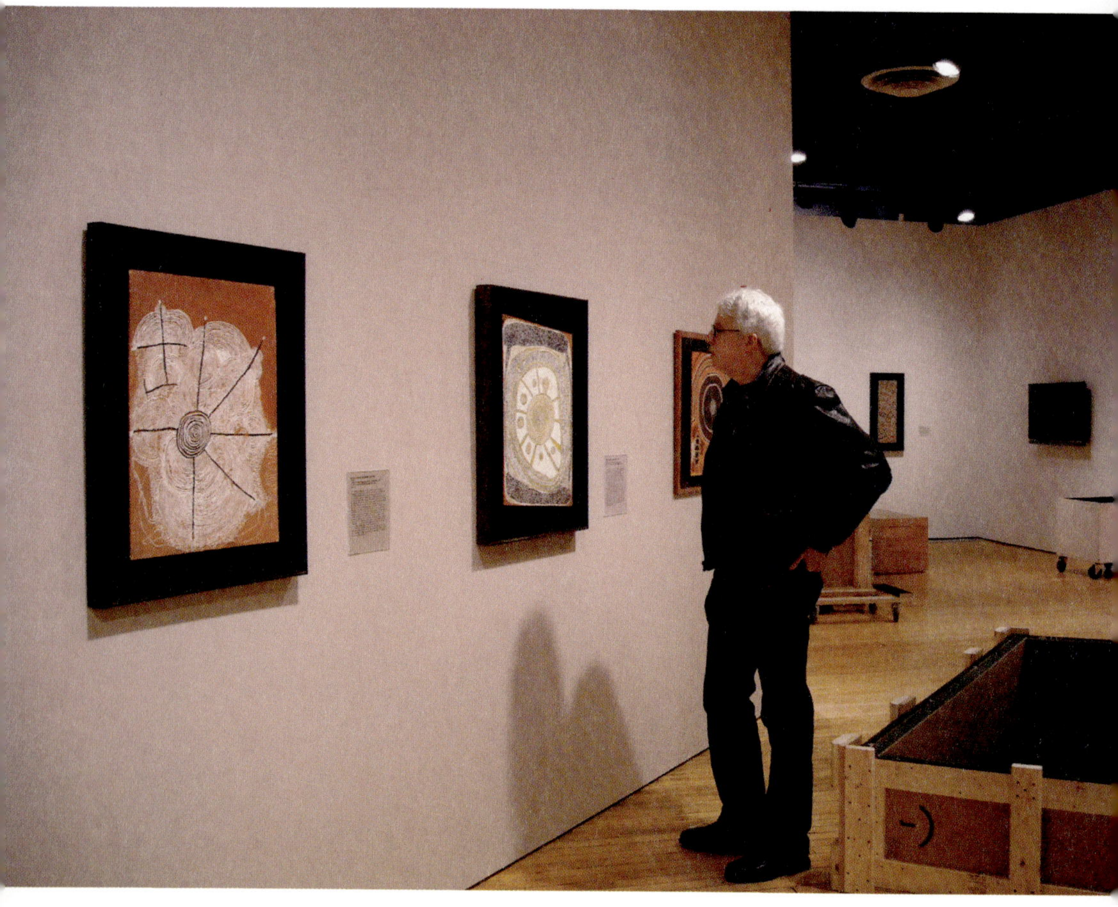

Discourse, Agency

Our conversation occurs, most audibly, between ourselves, as we respond to the invitation of the six paintings to engage them in conversation. Two on one, we interrogate each painting in turn, in order to hear them speak, so to speak. And each painting made its distinctiveness and power known as we faced it. These early works are small but have inescapable presence.

Furthermore, we are, as you will see, also in conversation with the many-voiced discourse that has grown up around them. The insights and ideas of previous interpreters (as well as information they have provided, and their value judgments) are in our minds as we look. They are alive in our conversation, talking to us about these paintings, sometimes about their experience of them when they were being made, or when they were later exhibited in a museum show, or when they were published.

Interpretations of the achievement at Papunya in the early 1970s have often turned on the question of agency, with the authenticity of each artistic statement as a subtext. They explicitly or implicitly ask the following questions: Who was, who were, the driving force; how was this force exercised; and how did it shape the art?

The first sustained writing on this art, which was the art educator Geoffrey Bardon's essays—unpublished in their original form, but used as the basis of chapters in his books *Aboriginal Art of the Western Desert* and *Papunya Tula: Art of the Western Desert*; and, with his brother, James Bardon, *Papunya: A Place Made after the Story*—moves between detailed descriptions of Bardon's role in every aspect of the painting process, short of applying brushstrokes with his own hand, and fulsome celebration of the independent inventiveness of most of the twenty-five or so men who regularly painted in the school rooms, the yard, his flat, and the Men's Painting Room (a World War II Nissen hut near the school, at times called "the Great Shed") during the early 1970s. A dedicated teacher committed to serving the interests of his students, their families, and these (as he soon discovered) remarkable men, Bardon veered in his writings between expressing the joys of creative confraternity and documenting the traumas of social isolation at Papunya—these writings are, as Una Rey puts it, "survivor memoirs" and all the more affective for that reason.[15] They are, as well, a remarkable effort at the witnessing of a phenomenon, as he was among the first non-Indigenous persons to recognize these paintings as an extraordinary gesture of transcultural translation on the part of the artists, one that required a complementary response.

Bardon's documentation remains an essential archive, not least because of the centrality it gives to painterly processes, to the extraordinarily inventive struggles of these men to translate their "sacred geographies," so mobile across time and space, onto the flat format of a transportable board. In his brilliant essay that prefaces *Papunya: A Place Made after the Story*, theorist Paul Carter lists the practical devices that Bardon introduced to channel the outpouring of creative energy triggered by the prospect of sharing their knowledge and, in their desperate circumstances, getting paid, however little, for doing so.[16] The first step required to prepare an artwork for circulation and sale is to decide that it is finished, ready to go. Carter claims that Bardon introduced this notion to the artists. More subtle constraints followed from the processes of recording each work when done. Photographing a painting, and identifying it on its back, does not strictly require deciding on its orientation, determining on top and bottom; done as a routine, however, it builds in orientation as an expectation. Labeling the work requires giving it a name. Linking the name to its subject matter, and explaining "the story" clearly, enhanced a painting's worth to those outside the community.[17]

One of the chapters in *Papunya: A Place Made after the Story* is titled "Subject Matter and Meaning and the Importance of the Idea of Story."[18] Elsewhere Bardon says, "For the Western Desert people there were usually no titles for the paintings, which were often named by me using conventional but also arbitrary terminologies. There is no physical horizon, only a conceptual one to enforce the certainty of a given meaning. A story was written so that word and image were the same; a painting was the worded image of the story."[19] The claim is not, obviously, that Bardon originated the great cycles and specific stories that constitute the Dreaming, nor the casual translation of them into English as "stories." Rather, he understood that the designs used in ceremony, and now being used in these paintings, were mnemonic pictographs, that (in Carter's words) "they employed a repertoire of *iconic* forms—concentric circles and lines—which (in the context of the story's telling) could be interpreted *conceptually*, as signifying the creative drama of the spiritual ancestors."[20] The Dreaming was and is replete with such dramas, which the men were anxious to convey and he to circulate for their benefit. "For the Western Desert painters and me, the making of each painting was like a theatrical and emotional act: I was concerned with the making of paintings with a Western Desert iconography and meaning to the exclusion of whitefella painting conventions, though with an efficient and artistically justified use of space."[21] He goes on to say that "the way the story was told became a preoccupation with me since I felt that intelligibility must involve a story's disposition, that its meaning be readily understood."[22]

As you will see, our conversation is animated by the recurrent recognition that, for all such attempts (however well intended) to impose these normalizing constraints, the creativity of the artists constantly exceeded them. A dispassionate reading of his texts shows that these excesses excited, even at times delighted, Bardon as much as they aroused his anxieties.

On a more general level, however, prioritizing Bardon over the artists within the Papunya Tula story fits a model that recurs often in studies of Indigenous art made in modern times: an emphasis on the pivotal role of a non-Indigenous mediator in the production of Indigenous "nontraditional," "hybrid," or "modernized" forms, ideas, and practices. This model pairs one non-Indigenous person—understood as acting largely alone, often alienated in important ways from their peers—alongside several Indigenous people, understood as embodying the culture of a community, sometimes an entire ethnicity. It attributes, at least in the origin phases of the story, roughly equal agency to both. It takes both to be necessary, but neither to be sufficient, as a cause of the entire phenomenon. There is, of course, an infinity of nuance in play in these situations, as close study of any of them will quickly reveal. One such nuance is the emergence of Indigenous individuals who take leading roles in negotiating with the colonizers.[23] As we shall soon see, this, too, occurred at Papunya.

Bardon's roles as a mediator were taken up by a succession of arts advisors and other supporters, unbroken to this day. All soundly based knowledge of the early years is also indebted to the recordkeeping and the occasional commentaries of advisors from these times, among them Pat Hogan, Dick Kimber, Peter Fannin, John Kean, Andrew Crocker, and Daphne Williams.[24] The continuity of Papunya Tula Artists Pty. Ltd., which Bardon, along with leading men, was instrumental in founding, is the actual and legal basis of this succession. Non-Indigenous managers work under the oversight of an all-Indigenous board. The subsequent prolific output of art from Papunya and other "decentered centers" in the region (not least Yuendumu, contemporaneously), its impact as a model in other remote communities (including those in the north focused on bark painting), and its chancy but persistent succession planning have echoes, with varying degrees of success, in what are now over one hundred Indigenous art centers across the continent. Indigenous art in Australia is buoyed by federal, state, and local government funding and also supported by an uneven yet persistent market. It is driven by wave after wave of Indigenous agency, in one remote community after another, and by individual artists and artist collectives in the towns and cities of Australia.[25] A system has emerged that eclipses similar ones elsewhere, including countries such as Canada that provide substantial support for their First Nations people. The decisive role of the Papunya painters in these developments became unarguable after exhibitions such as *Papunya: Genesis and Genius* in 2000.[26]

Sociologist Vivien Johnson's revisionary account, *Once Upon a Time in Papunya* (2010), responded to these factors as much as it did to her own direct and deep experience in the community, which began in 1980. She argues that the agency of the artists, in particular Kaapa Mbitjana Tjampitjinpa, was as least as consequential for the formation and the evolution of Papunya painting as that of Bardon—perhaps, she implies, more so. She shows that before Bardon's arrival several of the artists were actively painting in ways that pointed pathways beyond the "hybrid modernism" already prevalent in the region—beyond, that is, the Hermannsburg School of watercolorists who pursued the legacy of Albert Namatjira. Using art historical tools such as close stylistic analysis and a forensic tracking of documents, she suggests that a "School of Kaapa" can be discerned as an early substyle within the larger but still, at this point, emerging art movement. It is distinguished by its "style of miniaturised depictions of ceremonial grounds, objects and performances on plain backgrounds."[27] Several of these artists were among those who joined the Men's Painting Room. They brought with them their already-existing interests, painterly skills, and sets of social relations, especially the leadership of Kaapa and Old Mick Tjakamarra.

A further revision is evident in John Kean's research and writing, not least in his 2023 book, *Dot, Circle, and Frame: The Making of Papunya Tula Art.*[28] An art advisor at Papunya from 1977 to 1979, Kean argues that the artists Kaapa Tjampitjinpa, Tim Leura Tjapaltjarri, Clifford Possum Tjapaltjarri, and Johnny Warangula Tjupurrula were central to the greatest achievements of the early years, setting the framework, and the standards, for the subsequent flourishing, more so than any non-Indigenous actor, including Bardon. He locates the artists' inspiration in Namatjira's direct example as a money-making artist and as someone who "framed" sacred subjects in ways suitable for sharing with the noninitiated. Namatjira's well-known and widely valued landscapes, watercolors painted in the modified modernist style he learned from Rex Battarbee, featured not only tourist destinations.[29] The places he painted were also sacred sites; the natural features he highlighted were sacred beings.[30] Indigenous artists could see this clearly. Furthering the argument for this lineage, Kean unearthed two watercolor and pencil drawings dating from 1948 and attributed them to Namatjira. They both diagram markings on nine elliptically shaped ritual objects, with *yalka* (bush onion) symbols shown on the most prominent. The schematic layout and geometrical harmonies in both drawings anticipate the "School of Kaapa" style, while the symbolic infill and use of dotting in the second one prefigures these usages within Desert painting more generally.[31]

Kean also locates Papunya firmly within Central Australia rather than just the narrower Western Desert region, characterizing the broader area as "a dynamically evolving contact zone" not only between Indigenous and non-Indigenous inhabitants but also between diverse Aboriginal groups, each with "markedly different life experiences."[32] Three of the four key artists—Kaapa, Tim Leura, and Clifford Possum Tjapaltjarri—were Anmatyerr men and were cousins. All had been stockmen, were familiar with pastoralist modes of mapping, and were accomplished and successful carvers, familiar with marketing their wares. Johnny Warangkula, Mick Namarari Tjapaltjarri, and Wartuma (Charlie Tawara/Tjaruru) Tjungurrayi were Pintupi men who settled around Hermannsburg and then Haasts Bluff when they were children during the 1930s. Shorty Lungkarta Tjungurrayi and Uta Uta Tjangala were members of a more traditional group of Pintupi, ritually more mature when their families settled there in the late 1940s and 1950s. As we have noted, Papunya became central to the region during the 1960s, home to the Haasts Bluff Pintupi. In the following decades, these convergences triggered what Kean calls "the shiniest of shards from this collision of cultures."[33] It also became the staging post for people's efforts to return to their tribal lands—the outstation movement—which in turn spawned several large-scale, many-storied paintings. Kean says that, "seen in retrospect, the convergence of these events in 1971, signifies the transition from 'modern art,' associated with the 'assimilationist policy,' to 'contemporary art,' associated with Land Rights and 'self-determination.'"[34]

This view echoes the argument, first provocatively proposed by Ian McLean in 2010, that Papunya Tula art had an especially early, and powerful, role in demonstrating the contemporaneity of distinct differences that soon became definitive of global contemporary art in general.[35] Alert to the ways in which contemporary conditions precipitate the conjunction of disparate temporalities, McLean reads Papunya Tula as the conjunction of a belated "contact art" and late modernist avant-gardism, as a breakthrough moment in several convergent art histories, infused with Indigenous assertion of ancestral power, an artistic "rattling of the spears," the practice of calling up that power.[36] The placement of Papunya Tula painting has been a pivotal, ongoing topic in writing the history of Indigenous Australian art—indeed, of modern and contemporary Australian art as such.

Tjungunutja and *Kunatinpa*

The depth of Indigenous agency was asserted in the very name of the exhibition *Tjungunutja, from having come together*, held at the Museum and Art Gallery of the Northern Territory in 2017.[37] Bobby West Tjupurrula, son of one of the early painters at Papunya, and one of the Indigenous cocurators of the show, offered this name, explaining to the gallery curator Luke Scholes that his relatives (Pintupi newcomers and others) had negotiated a "shared identity" at Papunya through sharing knowledge of their Dreamings, their ceremonies, with other peoples there. At one point in the conversation, Bobby traces the path from ceremonial sharing and collaboration to painting. He turns to the other men and says,

> "Your group and us all *tjungurringu* [came together], from the west." Long Jack [Phillipus] replied: "Whole lot, right. Warlpiri, Anmatyerr, some Pitjantjatjarra, Pintupi. That's how they were, wasn't it." Bobby West: "That the one we call *Tjungunutja*." Sid Anderson: "*Palunya kula* [it is exactly that]. They were working together. *Tjungunutja*." Bobby: "When you made those boards, did those designs [stories] on the boards, self and self. Together you put them. Like *punyunyu* [novices], teaching them, East side, north side, west side, that one."[38]

This, he urged, was the foundation for the mutuality of the painters at Papunya. Importantly, this process had begun in the late 1960s, prior to the arrival of Bardon, and in parallel with the activities of Kaapa and other Anmatyerr artists. "After that," Bobby said, "after Tingarri, that's when they did the dot painting, body painting. Then they did that [Honey Ant Dreaming] mural at the school."[39] This is a claim that the outpouring of painting at Papunya was a by-product of the need for the different peoples obliged to live at Papunya—most of them on foreign land, displaced from their own country—to negotiate ways of living and working together: the outcome, first and foremost, of an Indigenous history.

Bobby West Tjupurrula and his cocurators also stressed another key element in how the painters thought about their work: it enabled the articulation of a relationship between themselves and the larger white/Australian society—with those they call *walypalas*. As Bobby said,

> At the conclusion of *punyunyu* [a ceremony for novices], we do what we call *kunatinpa* [ceremonial gift]. It's like when you go to church. You sit and listen and then when that *ingkata* [pastor] has finished speaking they ask you for one dollar or two dollars. The reason they ask for that money is because the *ingkata* has shared his knowledge.... We [the Indigenous curators], we're giving you our knowledge. This is the first time we're giving this knowledge in this way and you're giving us *kunatinpa*. We expect this, this is the way it should be.[40]

This is a call for the relationship to be one of hospitality, an exchange of gifts, a sharing of that which you can give for the benefit of both. We see our conversation as a modest effort, one among others, to meet this obligation.

Politics of the Gift

Hetti Perkins and the other Indigenous curators mentioned earlier have repeatedly drawn attention to the significance of Indigenous art and particularly Papunya Tula painting as expressing or articulating a claim or path to self-determination. In many remote communities, where conditions of scarcity prevail, the painting movement is a leading and reliable source—in some places, one of the few—of continuous income. As such, it is vital to the transfer of traditional knowledge between generations on which self-determination depends. That this has persisted for several decades, despite the abuses of exploiters, the vagaries of the art market, and the sensationalizing of its contradictions by racist elements in public media, is a testimony to the commitment of all involved.[41]

While the political agency articulated in these works, their claims over country and the value of their own culture in the face of assimilative pressures, might have seemed a barrier to their recognition in some discourses of art, lessening their "autonomy" as artworks, it has been central to "the work of art" as the painters have seen it, to the cultural, social, and political work that it does—not least, facilitating a return to the traditional lands of those exiled at Papunya.[42] In this last, political purpose, the painting movement has been, and continues to be, a vital enabling factor.

More broadly, the nationwide recognition accorded these paintings has led to greater knowledge and acceptance of Indigenous presence and creativity. Their imagery, as circulated on Land Rights posters, has increased understanding of Indigenous relations to country, and this has leveraged philanthropic support for such needed services as the establishment of an

Indigenous-controlled organization to provide remote local dialysis treatment for the epidemic of kidney failure in Central Australia.[43] Indigenous protocols expressed in terms of intellectual or cultural property—about who owns the paintings and what can be shown or must be restricted—have also entered legal and museological domains once dominated by Western property regimes. This trajectory allows us to see that the hopes of the older people that the revelation of their knowledge would establish stronger relations with those to whom it is revealed (*yutinu*) or given (*yungu*) have, to a meaningful degree, been realized. Despite the fears of many who foresaw cultural destruction following from the sharing of this art, the painting movement has, in many remote communities, instead become a vehicle of self-determination.

The Aestheticist Diversion

Hovering to one side of these debates about how to respond to these artworks is the wish to have no debate at all. In the exhibitions he organized in the early 1980s, one Papunya arts advisor, Andrew Crocker, sought to "migrate these paintings from ethnography to art." Each opened with this wall label: "Much could be said of the genesis of the Western Desert School and also of its role in the artists' society. I think that for the purposes of this exhibition the paintings should be allowed to exercise their own aesthetic appeal and that explanations of content and symbolism be best kept to a minimum."[44] These sentiments echo in some presentations of recent work by Indigenous artists who, it is urged, are by now so versed in the languages of contemporary art that they have transcended their obligations to kin and country and have become, for example, "simply painters: some of the finest abstract painters this planet has ever seen."[45] While true, there is nothing simple about it. Such attitudes misunderstand abstraction as an artistic approach, the diverse languages of contemporary art, and what essentially propels these men and women to make the kind of art that they do. It is a wish to assimilate this art into categories conventional within Western art but presumed to be universal. These Indigenous Australian artists are not making a peripheral contribution to the history of Western modernism. Within the broader range of negotiations that we have described, they are introducing to the world a set of painterly practices that are at once traditional, modern, and contemporary.[46]

Seeing, Speaking, Silence

Each step in the evolution of the discourse we have just sketched—from Papunya itself to the global contemporary art world—enriches and expands the overall picture while at the same time filling in the details of who did what, when, and with which effect. Being familiar with these and several other important contributions, we were excited to test their insights against the evidence of the actual artworks that generated them. In the expanding body of writing about this art, there is, too, a growing interaction between disciplinary approaches, a more subtle weaving of voices, in the discussion of the artworks themselves. But sustained analyses of individual works are still rare. Sharing the story and then showing how the artist tells it remains the default mode.

Thirteen paintings from the Wilkerson collection were on show at the Australian Consulate-General's residence. Having decided to focus on the earliest works, we centered the following conversation on six that were painted in 1971 and 1972, with comparative remarks about others made at the time and since. Most of the others in the exhibition were painted in subsequent years.[47]

This conversation emerged during the pandemic, in New York City (of all places), and from a twenty-five-year history of dialogue between us. While deeply influenced by Indigenous artists and curators, and their knowledge shared with us over the years, we can only articulate what we know and what we can see, speaking together in front of these paintings. We do so in the hope that our conversation might add something to the ongoing discourse, bridge some of its interpretive gaps, as we look closely at a selection of these artworks, striving to unpack how they were made, when, why, and with what impact during those crucial early years of what became a remarkably diverse and resilient, continuously self-replenishing art movement.

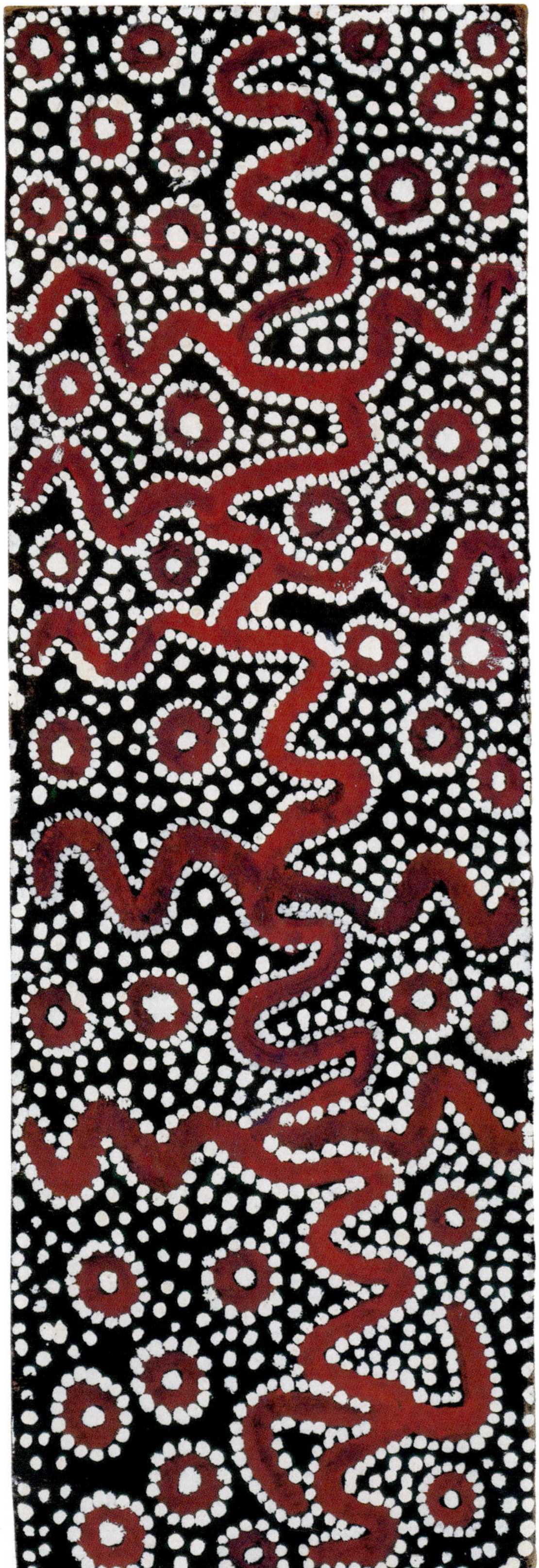

1 THE ETERNAL RECURRENCE OF ORIGINS

Kingsley Tjungurrayi, *Stars, Rain, and Lightning at Night*, 1971

Terry Smith Let's begin with the earliest painting in the Wilkerson collection, now known as *Stars, Rain, and Lightning at Night*, by Kingsley Tjungurrayi. It was part of the first consignment of boards by artists at Papunya to the Stuart Art Centre in Alice Springs. In Pat Hogan's notes, taken as she received the paintings at the center, the roundels are labeled as "stars at night" and the wavy lines as "lightning."[1] According to Geoffrey Bardon, it was made before or around May 1971 and impressed him as archetypal.[2]

I think that Geoff (whom I knew in the 1990s) was speaking as an abstract painter, an artist trained in the protocols of modernist abstraction, which include many modes for producing forms that work relative to each other within the limits of a format of a given size. Yet these forms can also, at the same time, work as abstract equivalents of natural phenomena, as shapes existing in the space created inside the painting itself. And they can conjure

1.1 Kingsley Tjungurrayi, *Stars, Rain, and Lightning at Night*, before May 1971. Synthetic polymer and enamel paint on composition board, 70.63 × 23.18 cm. © Estate of the artist | Aboriginal Artists Agency Ltd.

archetypes, the most fundamental elements of human understanding, according to psychoanalyst Carl Jung and arts educator Herbert Read, whose writing Bardon studied.

So, for Bardon, something at once familiar but also very different is occurring here, in these very early boards. He is seeing abstract forms become figures. And figures acting as if they were abstract forms. No wonder he got so excited and announced that Papunya painting was a breakthrough in the history of art!

I would like to start from the most visually obvious, most distinctive elements of paintings such as this one: the dots, in space, and around each shape. What imaging work are they doing? Where do they come from as a presentational device? Neither Geoff Bardon nor Pat Hogan mention the dotting in their notes on these paintings. Perhaps they just took them for granted as a highlighting device. Their focus at this point, Bardon's especially, was on the symbolic forms, as a system, a language, of graphic motifs. He obviously appreciated that the meaning of a concentric circle, say, could shift depending on its place in the story, but mostly, when it comes to naming the painting, he goes for a one-to-one equivalence between the sign and the signified; the totality of meaning is—suddenly—all there. No ambiguity, no double meanings, no layers of meaning. Everything seems utterly simple and straightforward, as if it's already formed as a fully coherent visual statement.

Although, in this painting, it must be said that the statement *is* a relatively simple one. As if it were an early instantiation of an idea, like setting out an alphabet as a sequence of letters.

It is also rather roughly delineated, using enamel paint, house paint that the artist found around the settlement, applied straight to the hardboard, itself a found material. So different from most of the other paintings we will discuss; they were made using dedicated art materials: fine sable hairbrushes and synthetic polymer or acrylic paints, applied to composition board, everything supplied by Bardon, the art teacher—who does not seem to be very present here, in these early months of 1971.

But I might be mythologizing about origins. These impressions might simply be an effect of someone making a familiar mark—a sign with an already-given meaning, an icon within a well-known, millennia-long iconography—on an unfamiliar surface. We need to talk about this a bit more. . . .

Fred Myers Okay. Actually, in Bardon's catalog in *A Place Made after the Story*, his reproduction flips the painting vertically from the way it is hung here in New York. And Vivien Johnson, in her book *Once Upon a Time at*

Papunya, turns it sideways.[3] I don't think that these orientations change its meaning, however....

TS A good reminder that we can take nothing for granted, as we stand here looking at this painting, not least how we are standing as we look!

After all, in the desert, ground paintings are approached from all sides, and the markings on bodies are meant to be seen from many angles, in different light conditions, usually on a moving body. The designs, as such, are evocations of ideas, places, ancestors, events—they have no fixed orientation in space, relative to some abstract observer, of the kind we presume when we visit galleries or exhibitions such as this.

FM Yes. The larger circles with the dots around them are said to signify the stars. The main shapes (in pink), the jagged form, are a conventional symbol for lightning but down toward the bottom, as we see it, there is a figure, the semicircular shape, which is the conventional Western Desert sign of a person sitting, apparently what we might call a "rain man," an ancestral or Dreaming figure identified with rain and lightning.

I have witnessed a Rain Dreaming ceremony from a different part of the desert, and the iconography of the body decoration associated with it, the signs painted and placed on the bodies of performers, is pretty much identical to the red shapes in this painting. The same imagery is repeated in many other paintings associated with the ancestral or mythological stories of rain and lightning.

There's no annotation in Bardon's books about the dotting, which I guess seemed unremarkable to him, but the outlining dotting [around the stars and lightning] is characteristic of many examples of body painting and ground painting, where the dots are used to enclose or to draw out a feature. So, these symbols are clearly iconographic.

Kingsley is misdescribed in a lot of the accounts as being an Arrernte/Anmatyerr man and part-Afghan, but, according to Vivien Johnson, who really did more research on the records, he's from Ilpili, which is in the Ehrenberg Range, at the eastern edge of Pintupi country.[4] He's a Luritja/Pintupi man, a Tjungurrayi. The Papunya Census from 1961 has him as born in 1917, in the Kintore Range, out west of Ilpili. And Kintore [Walunguru] isn't far from Kalipinynga, which is sometimes spelled Kalipinypa. It's the Rain/Lightning Dreaming place of Johnny Warangkula's painting, which we will talk about later. The proximity of these two places suggests he might also have been a custodian of this Dreaming story and therefore possesses the right to paint it.

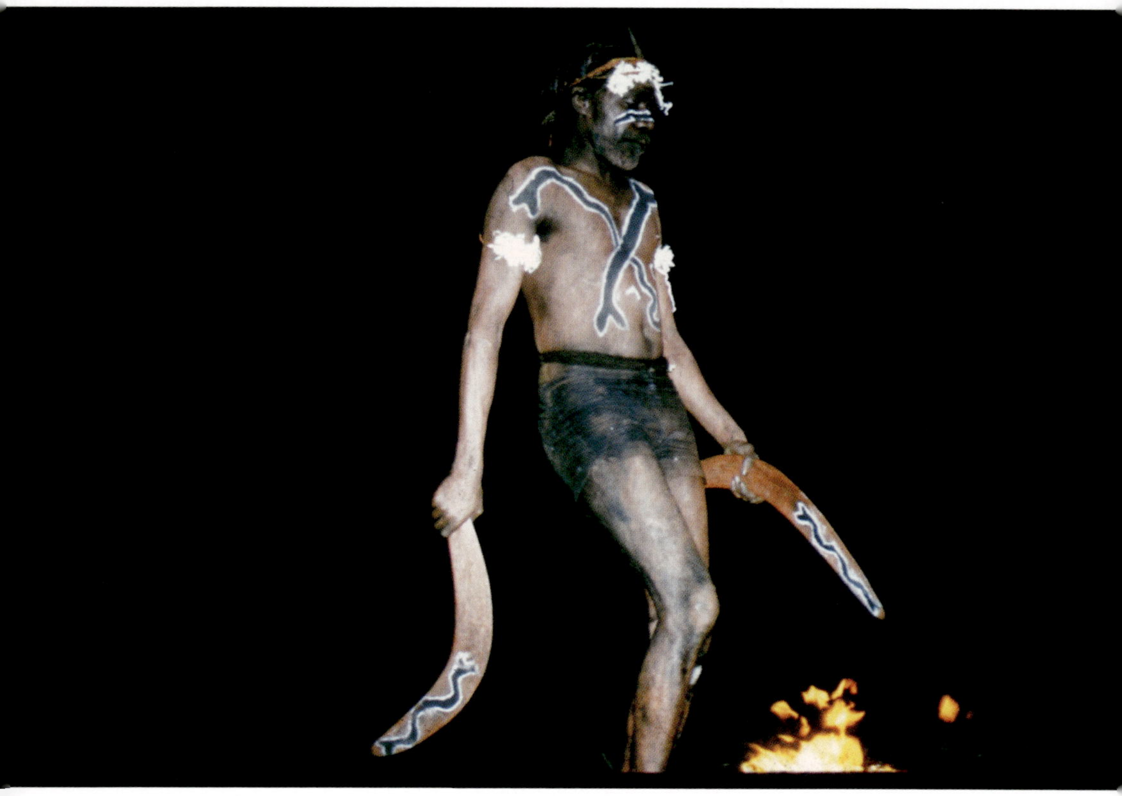

1.2 Jeffrey James Tjangala performs a Rain Dreaming dance, Yayayi, Northern Territory, 1974. Photograph by Fred Myers. Used with permission of the family of Tjangala.

This makes me think that the painting, one of the earliest in the movement, is about the story associated with *that* place, or—if you will—simply a different representation of Kalipinypa.

I think I knew him, actually. His name, as I knew it, was Nabo. He obviously was more engaged with white people than many of the other painters within this early group. Given where he came from, he would have had earlier and longer periods of contact than some of the later Pintupi. We could assume, given the length of time of his engagement with non-Indigenous people, that he had seen more things. Clifford Possum Tjapaltjarri and Kaapa Tjampitjinpa, for example, also from earlier waves of contact, had seen comic books, but not taken them in as much. As it turned out, Kingsley only painted for a short time, becoming more interested in other things.

TS Yet some aspects of the way he has made this painting strike me as a little bit unusual. The dots around the figures do the intensifying, as you said, and then they are mostly randomly inserted in the black or "night" spaces. But then he has marked the edges of the board with rows of dots. This seems to indicate an awareness that the overall image, the central configuration, should stay within the physical limits of whatever you are painting on. I know that delineating borders is common in body marking, and I think in sand painting, but not so often done with dots. This seems an unusual act of visual coherence-making. A formalist critic would call it "respecting the frame."

FM You're right: it is not common. Yet this is 1971. He is likely to have had some visual literacy anyway, possibly some education at Haasts Bluff, at the Lutheran mission. He could've been looking at things like printed papers with hymns, with illustrations of Jesus and so on. Also, they had film strips of Bible stories.

TS All right. The other thing I noticed is that across the top the four stars are regularly placed, then there's a sort of pairing of stars all the way down into the bottom of the space where the disposition of the elements is much looser. Is this because they are proximate to the rain man, implying a different dynamic in the field around him? What do you think, Fred?

FM I think he's just filling the space in.

TS Oh, okay. My final thought is about the way he has painted the lightning. If you take it as a coherent single shape, there is some rhythm in repetition of the horizontal bars, but they wobble so much the overall sense is of a connected but also crazily explosive figure. Like several snakes become one. Or rapidly flowing water. It seems to evoke rhizomatic spreading as such. Or perhaps he is showing us many lightning strikes at once, but somehow rendered as one connected phenomenon. It certainly conveys the crackling, electric energy of a lot of lightning occurring simultaneously across a vast space. Something many of us have experienced. Usually followed by thunder and rain. No wonder this painting was once named *Storm*. There are explosive images like this in some of the rock paintings up north, in certain sorcery figures, but I don't know many other figures as wild as this one.

FM You find such figures in body decoration quite often. The ones I saw involved covering the torso with red ochre mixed with fat, and then using a paste of water and ground charcoal, laying on the jagged shape of lightning to fill up the front torso, adding a white outline, made with ashes and water, to enclose or mark off the lightning. In the ceremony I remember, the men danced with the decorations in front of the flickering fire at night, creating the flash or shimmering effect, like a strobe, emanating as a kind of ancestral power.

But the body does not offer as much space. So, I think at issue here is that this board offered an unusually shaped space. It looks like it's perfect for a lightning image. It's really long, relative to a torso.

Yet the craziness, as you call it, or wildness, might simply be adjustments to the given space. I mean, he starts out at a certain scale and then realizes, "Oh, I've got more to go," you know?

TS Your photographs of the Rain Dreaming ceremonies at Yayayi show that the body painters weren't afraid to use considerable variation in rendering the icon, perhaps responding to body shape.

So, we can't presume that Kingsley Tjungurrayi was thinking about the whole area from top to bottom before he started on it.[5] Nor of a fixed, conventional form, like a slightly larger dot for a star. Obviously, he must retain the general look of the sign for lightning, but it seems as if this rendition of it kind of grew as it went along. If you look closely, you can see where he replenishes his paint, where the color changes slightly, a richer pink appears.

FM You can see that he has painted the lightning figure first. We have to imagine the whole painting without any dots whatsoever. After all, that's the normal order of these paintings. Basic design first, intensifying dots next, then infill.

TS Right. So, we chose to talk about this painting first because it is the earliest in the Wilkerson collection, as close as we can get, standing here in New York, to an artifact of the temporal origins of the art movement "miracle" at Papunya. Our conversation has made me aware that I, at least, began from a premise that made a myth out of origins. Obviously, the imagery Kingsley used has been original since the Lightning Man appeared. It's original each time it recurs. That includes Kingsley's efforts, early in 1971, to fit this imagery to this board—so that others, at and beyond Papunya, could see it, could sense its power.

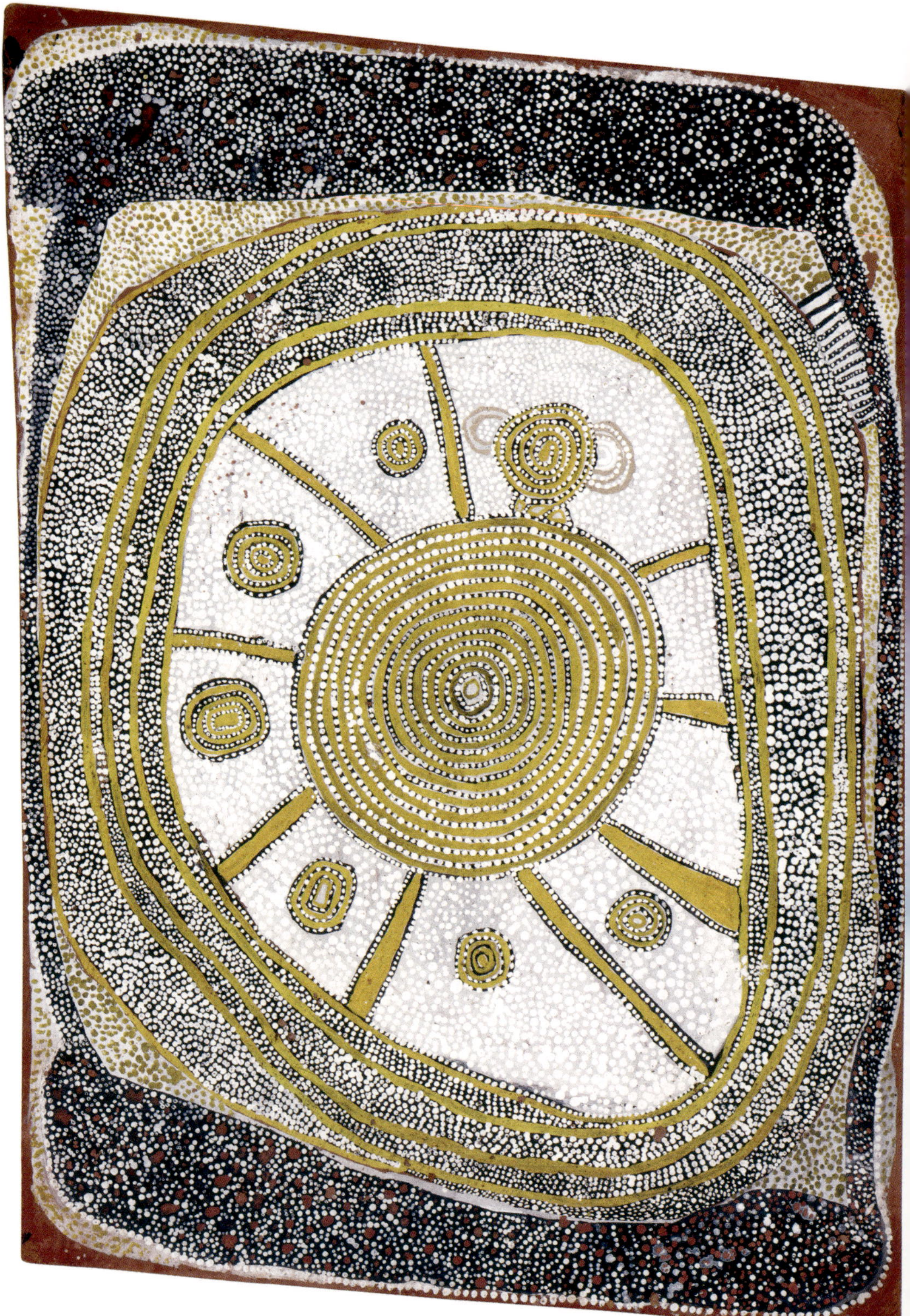

THE CEREMONY IS THE PLACE

The Past Is the Present

Shorty Lungkarta Tjungurrayi, *Classic Pintupi Water Dreaming*, 1972

TS For me, when I begin to look at this painting, I am struck by the contrast between the importance of the subject matter—"classic Pintupi Water Dreaming," as the title says—and the scrappy nature of the support. . . . This distorted rectangle, typical of the bits of Masonite—as we used to call composition board in those days—that were useless for their main purpose: as interior wall cladding, kitchen cupboard doors, and the like. This support is a long way from those used by professional painters in the cities. It reinforces the mythology that, at the birth of this art movement, the men would paint on anything they could lay their hands on.

Yet we know that by now, August of 1972, Bardon was supplying them with good quality acrylic paint, of the kind used in art classes in the school. In the background to some of the photographs of the artists at work, you can see a bench with paint cans and brushes, plus a few paintings, clustered in a place assigned to each artist. Bardon seems to have printed out their names, taped them to the back wall, to divide the bench into sections. Just like a school art

2.1 Shorty Lungkarta Tjungurrayi, *Classic Pintupi Water Dreaming*, August 1972. Synthetic polymer/powder paint on composition board, 62.23 × 41.59 cm. © Estate of the artist | Aboriginal Artists Agency Ltd.

room. [Michael] Jensen's photographs show that Shorty was using a fine watercolor brush. So was Johnny Warangkula, sitting right next to him, painting his masterly *Water Dreaming at Kalipinypa*.[1]

FM *Classic Pintupi Water Dreaming* is one of my favorites in the Wilkerson collection. Shorty Lungkarta Tjungurrayi was one of my closest interlocutors, my *tjamu* [grandfather]. His tireless and generous instruction was crucial to my understanding of Pintupi painting and so much else of their lives.

Benjamin emphasizes that this painting was done in August 1972, during an extraordinarily rainy period. He attributes the "topic" of the painting to that historical circumstance.[2]

TS Yes, there was a strong tendency, when these paintings first appeared in galleries and museums in the 1980s, to read them as landscapes, painted at a particular time and place, with what was happening to the natural phenomena as at least part of their meaning. Perhaps this was the aspect most accessible to non-Indigenous viewers.

FM Interpreting this painting as primarily a depiction of weather or rain misses a fundamental dimension of the aesthetics at work. Neither Bardon's notes nor Pat Hogan's suggest that this might be a painting concerned with a place, but Dick Kimber does point to an important site in Shorty's country, Lampintjanya, his birthplace.[3] I know from my own documentation of his other paintings that this place was a frequent subject from 1973 to 1975. And that he visited it often before he left the foraging life in the bush in 1948.[4] It is, therefore, not only a place whose contours and geographical qualities were profoundly part of his lived experience in his country [*ngurra*]; it is also a place with an ancestral [Dreaming, *Tjukurrpa*] story. In this sense, it is an example of what I have called an aesthetics of "doubling."[5]

TS There was also a related tendency to understand these paintings as depictions of places that could be seen from a viewing position equivalent to, but not the same as, vanishing-point perspective in the European visual tradition. So, they were described as "maps," or areas seen from the air, as if you traveled over them in an airplane. God's-eye view. It makes more sense, however, to understand the viewpoint as that over a ground painting, or of looking at a body in ceremony. This angle is translated by someone painting, at arm's length, with the support on their lap, or lying flat on the ground. Photographs show the artist squatting on the floor with this board in front of him. You can imagine him turning it slowly, in a circular fashion, as he inserts the dots.

I am fascinated by how the traditional imagery of this place takes possession of this oddly shaped board. The basic structure is two horizontal bars (above and below) linked by vertical lines that enclose a set of circular shapes. We will see the same framework in other paintings, like Charlie Tarawa's [Wartuma's] painting known as *The Trial*, which we will talk about next, which uses it to convey a sense of enclosure or of being entrapped. In this painting, the opposite seems to be happening: all the elements seem to burst with a lively energy, conveyed mostly by the contrast between the white dots and the yellow lines—a rarely used dominant color at this time. The black framing within each side is similarly enlivened by lots of red dots.

It is a remarkable example of the way these artists worked to establish a format familiar to them—it comes from painting the torso for ceremony—within the limits of a standardized shape. Or, in this case, a distorted version of the usual rectangles or squares.

FM Certainly, this design of a large circle inside a framing of two bars (top and bottom) resonates with some templates of painting on the body. In this case, the annotations lead us to understand the central roundel as "a waterhole surrounded by soaks (represented by small sets of concentric circles) with little creeks flowing into it from a larger watercourse that surrounds. The darker forms at each end represent hills."[6]

Kimber surmises that the creeks were formed by the movements of ancestral snakes and that the black ovals represent hills promoting rainstorm runoff into the claypan. The red overdotting, he writes, may represent *mungilypa* [the seed-bearing plant *Tecticornia verrucosa*], abundant after rains.[7]

In Shorty's experience, Lampintjanya was a place he and his family visited after rains, to exploit the abundant water and seeds as resources to support larger-than-usual gatherings of people. It is, therefore, an image of abundance and sociality, of gathering of families. But it is also an ancestral story, one connected to the ancestral snakes identified with the Dreaming at this place. The two men whom Bardon sees denoted by the semicircles around one concentric circle inside the central area are very likely the Dreaming ancestors of two men Shorty knew well: George Tjangala and Left Hand Frank [whose name was Mungilnga, after the name of the seed plant].[8] The ancestors were brothers, as were the two men named, who were digging and pursuing two carpet snakes toward a hole, and they began to quarrel at this place over shares of the seedcakes made from *mungilypa*, and threw dirt at each other before escalating to sorcery or magical attacks through incantation.

There may be yet another layer of meaning in play here. To me, it is hard not to see in this image—a circle surrounding a smaller set of concentric circles but connected by the extension of rectilinear forms from inside to outside—an evocation of a circular ritual headdress mounted on the head of a performer, and projected outward onto a bigger circular form (made of grass and branches packed into a circle, bound by hair string and decorated). This would make the painting a representation of a watery place and its geography as in the artist's lived experience and, *at the same time*, an evocation of the ceremony that reenacts the ancestral presence that made this place. There seem to be multiple representations within representations.

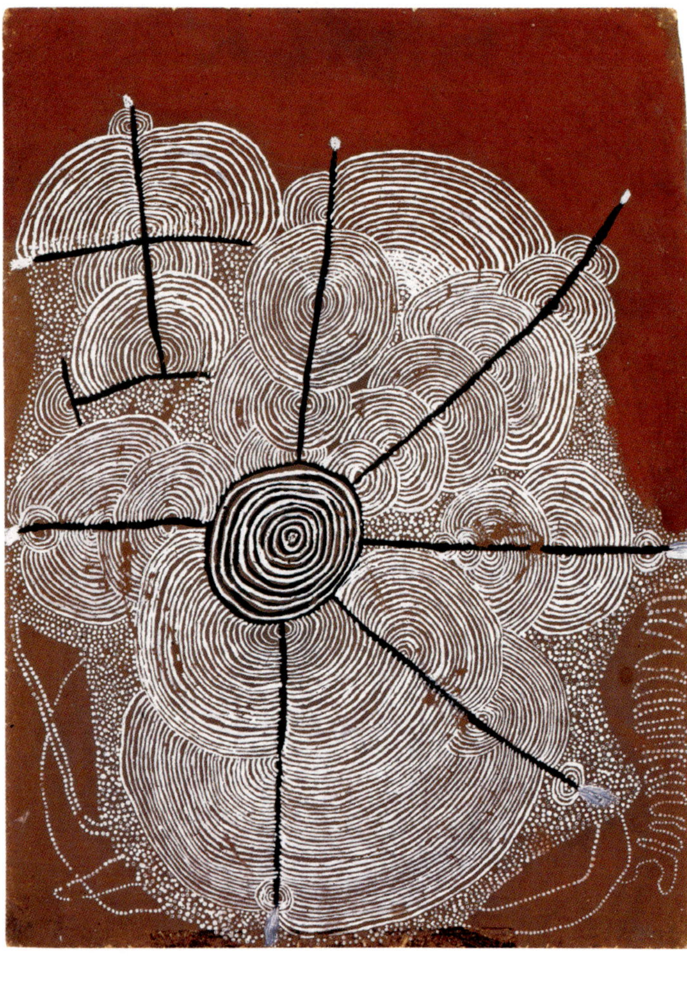

2.2 Shorty Lungkarta Tjungurrayi, *Children's Water Dreaming (Version 2)*, May–July 1972. Synthetic polymer paint on composition board, 61.6 × 44.45 cm. © Estate of the artist | Aboriginal Artists Agency Ltd.

TS Your suggestion that there is a hint of a headdress in this painting made me want to take a quick detour from our six paintings and look at another painting by Shorty that is in the collection. I think it might help us understand this one better. Its title is *Children's Water Dreaming (Version 2)*, and it was done a few months earlier, between May and July 1972. It is on a similar-sized board, not quite so wonky in shape, but also abraded around the edges. He uses only black and white paint, straight onto the surface, which is in the standard brown color as it comes from its manufacturer.

FM Yes. I believe this painting, like the one called *Classic Pintupi Water Dreaming*, also represents Lampintjanya, and again we have the features identified with the waterhole, the creeks, and flowing water. It suggests a similar combination of the lived experience of water flowing at the place *and* its ancestral/ritual foundation. The painting is, therefore, both ancestral and present. The semicircular patterns are identified by Bardon's notes as "water running in the creek."[9] At this level, the painting simply depicts the landscape as it was created by events of the Dreaming. Lampintjanya is a claypan, with water running down from a rocky hill. The painting was indeed made when Central Australia was deluged with rain, and the semicircles remind us of how claypans and dry waterbeds look when filled by water. The black lines delineate the creeks while the semicircular pattern depicts windblown waves on the full claypan. Shorty reveals Lampintjanya as the lived place of floodwaters but also as formed by the actions of the Dreaming.

TS To me, this is like a sketch for the concept of the painting we are discussing, its conceptual diagram, as it were. It is so clear about its own process. Like a sand painting, it is built from the inside out—in that case, you work inside out so you don't muck up the work you have done, laying in those piles of ochres, of crushed vegetation and bird feathers. Here, the central circle is given, in black lines, six of which then radiate outward. Inside the central circle, white lines reinforce the black ones already there, highlighting its concentricity, ratcheting up the intensity. White lines then echo from the center, at some places as smaller concentrations, at one (lower right) section as loops within that section. Some loops are quite small and have two dots inside them. A smaller black figure, cross-shaped (sort of), appears at the upper left. Scattered white dots underlie the whole shape, as if it was a place with identifiable limits. Yet each black line has a white tuft at the tip. And lines of white dots dangle loosely between the lower arms.

Is he simply translating a well-known body-painting design on to this board, as he does in the painting we just discussed? More likely, perhaps, it's a sand painting design.

FM Pintupi were not as active as Warlpiri when it comes to ground paintings. . . .

TS Oh, I am closest to Warlpiri, through Paddy Japaltjarri Sims, where that is the presumption. Ground paintings were, more often than not, the traditional sources of the designs and of the compositions of their paintings made for showing to others.[10]

So, in this case, if we are not talking about body designs, or sand paintings, or markings on ritual objects as the template, what are the other options? One is to improvise a design on a surface that offers a kind of nonspace. So that the design stands in its own form, as it were. Yes, it has a color and a texture. I suppose the brown of the board made me think of it as connoting earth or sand. Like the other boards painted black for night or red for a sort of sacred space, evoking the sun, or a body, or red sand. Another option could be that the artist is simply painting on a surface to hand, taking it as offering a neutral ground on which the figure can be placed.

I also see this as a sketch for his later art, for the kind of wild, whirling, concentric circle paintings he would soon make, so impressively. It is the second version, his second attempt at this solution: the first we know only from a black and white photograph in Bardon's book. It has the same two components, except that the smaller one is not given as a "cross" shape. It is just a smaller cluster of concentric circles off to one side, although it is connected by one of the radial lines, possibly what he labels a "ceremonial stick."[11]

We know that improvisation was the name of the game at this stage. The artists had been warned off picturing secret, sacred imagery. Some responded by choosing subjects that were not sacred, or were at least publicly shareable, as women's stories and children's stories were presumed to be. Bardon says he urged them down this path, to help educate the children and in the interests of harmony between the different groups.[12] Thus the titles of many paintings made during these months: *Children's Dreaming of the Bush Banana*, or *Naughty Boy's Dreaming*. Henry has recently had some interesting things to say about these titles. . . .

FM Yes, Henry Skerritt wrote about this in the catalog we edited together, *Irriṯitja Kuwarri Tjungu / Past and Present Together*. The titles of some of the paintings by Mick Namarari Tjapaltjarri, as annotated by Bardon, seemed to us to be misleading. In order to ensure the men were painting stories that could be circulated or seen by anybody (without restriction for ritual content), we know that Bardon asked for "children's paintings"—which he communicated as "*chi chi tjuckatjuk*"—a rendering of the words *tjitji tjukutjuku* [small children] in Pintupi, implying some association with children. I went back to old notes I had made about the stories at this place. Henry argues that the title *Family Bush Tucker Dreaming*, given by Bardon to one of Mick Namarari's paintings, is "infantilizing" because the story actually is of the transgressive sexual intercourse with a sleeping Snake Woman (known as Kutungu) by uninitiated "boys" [*tjitji*] at the place named Muruntji. It is a story that is regarded with some humor but also as an action eliciting a harsh and angry response from Kutungu. Namarari painted this story more explicitly at other times, and he had some rights to the story. I think Henry is making a brilliant and specific argument for renaming these paintings for the place, not as telling generic children's stories. Indeed, Henry suggests that the men may have understood Bardon to be asking for paintings based on stories *about* children, not *childlike* stories.[13]

The "children's story" that we are discussing now is one of the paintings that Bardon directed to be painted in this framework. If it is Lampintjanya, which Shorty did frequently paint, the ancestral story does involve two boys—uninitiated males, and thus *tjitji*—who were active at this claypan site and are identified with it. Whether we can see their presence in this painting is uncertain, but Shorty named them in discussing other paintings of this site when I documented them with him.

There is another dimension, now pretty much lost. When Bardon and some others documented paintings, they did not hear reference—as I frequently did—to the *living representatives* of the ancestral figures in these paintings. Knowing this, having references to it in the contemporaneous notes, would add to our possible understanding of other affective dimensions of these images. These men, for example, were Shorty's brothers-in-law [*marutju*], and they had overlapping lives as youngsters in the bush.

TS We are moving into the second, more challenging, option for these artists when they received pushback against showing secret, sacred content: do so without using sacred icons, do it covertly, by implication, in ways that cannot be reduced to icons or recognizable figures.

So many of the early paintings are struggling with this dilemma. I see Shorty Lungkarta, in this painting, as accepting a comforting title, but at the same time striving, struggling, to find ways of suggesting the deeper content—without showing it. The politics of the secret, as Kimber says.[14]

The poetics of secrecy, we might add.

FM Right. The crosslike shape in this painting—which is simply identified as *puturru* [hair string] in Bardon's documentation and superficially as the wooden cross used for spinning human hair into string—is almost certainly also a hidden or obscured representation of a profoundly secret ritual object. Such an object is identified with the ancestral figures of the place; it is carried in ceremony. It is an object "hidden" in this painting, in the same way that the Dreaming [*Tjukurrpa*] is not accessible directly in the everyday. It is an obfuscation, similar to the way access to knowledge is restricted in Pintupi social life, restricted to those properly initiated.

It may also be understood as "hidden" in the way that restricted objects and knowledge are managed in ceremonies. Often, a sacred object, known to be present, is briefly shown or deliberately obscured, so that observers can only catch a glimpse. The knowledge is "given," in this sense, but also partially withheld. The ancestor is present but not entirely revealed. This is a really important ritual technique. These senior men are very familiar with it. I think that it was natural to them to manage the imagery in the paintings in the same sort of way.

So, in this painting, there is something very powerful, to me, in the overlapping or swirling concentric semicircles (very typical of Shorty's later paintings) which are said to be the swirling water, but they also resonate visually with the way the hair string is wound when it is spun on a crosslike pair of sticks and used to make actual ceremonial objects. During the ceremony, these were carried by actors or worn as head ornaments. We can speak about them only in the most general terms.[15]

TS Aha! You are explaining, perhaps, something that really puzzles me about how the ritual object that is sketched schematically in the upper left, the crosslike shape, relates to the configuration suggested by the main black lines, annotated as the "big waterhole" radiating "little creeks." I am struggling to understand how the smaller shape is situated relative to the larger one. Does it grow out of the larger one, like a spin-off from its dynamic energies? That would locate everything we see on the same plane. A self-creating plane.

Or are we looking at two objects, indicating two performers, as might be imagined considering the back story of the "two boys"? If we imagine these two together within a narrative taking place in time and across space, we can begin to picture a Water Dreaming ceremony in the center, with the ritual object having arrived at the ceremonial grounds.

I notice that the radiating black lines of the main shape also have tufts at their ends, especially the middle and lower arms. Like bird feathers or fur chalked with white ochre. He has touched up three of them with blue paint. Could they also be an evocation of a ceremonial structure? And of an ancestor? And of a present-day performer—like him? I recall that you write about him as being an exceptional performer.[16]

In his notes on version 1 of this painting, I see that Bardon says "possibly ceremonial sticks" about these lines.[17] In this first version, they have more pronounced end circles and tufts.

FM Yes, Bardon was being cautious, careful not to disclose secret information. We are in the same situation.

TS Whatever way we read the two main elements, taken together they fuse into a whole, with many bustling, bursting points of energy, constantly renewing themselves. Swirling in and out. Looking at this painting from an art historical point of view, we can feel the key components of what he will do as an artist coming into being.

That's why I see it as a sketch, a prefiguration of later paintings. Let's look again at the interior section of *Classic Pintupi Water Dreaming*. The same spoke-and-wheel configuration is right there. Yet it is taken a step further by adding a circular form that constrains the central energies somewhat but has its own dynamism, spinning the whole composition. Then, as we noted, all this energy is framed by the lozenge shapes at the top and bottom, themselves joined. So, in sum, this body painting template contains the freely drawn improvisation we saw in *Children's Water Dreaming*, so-called.[18]

As you said earlier, Shorty is showing the presence of the ancestors who made this place during ceremony—showing us how they did so, and the continuing effects of what they did. The past is the present: the place is the ceremony.

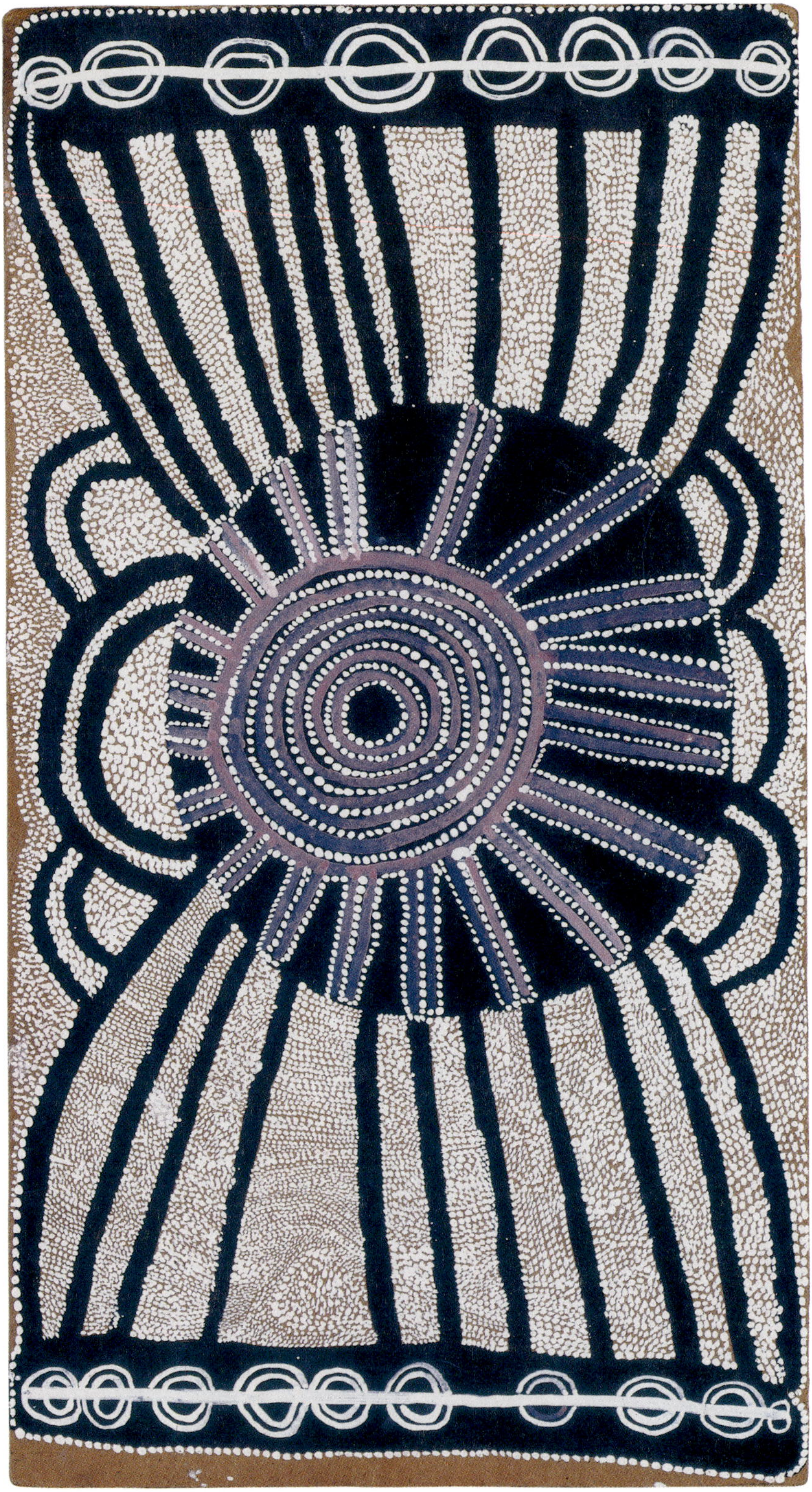

3 THE ICY SPIRIT

The Structure of Punishment

Wartuma (Charlie Tarawa/Tjaruru) Tjungurrayi, *The Trial*, 1972

FM This painting by Charlie Tarawa, done in 1972, known as *The Trial*, is a truly exceptional piece of work.

TS Absolutely.

FM It was on the poster of the *Icons of the Desert* exhibition in 2009, when it was at the Grey Art Gallery at New York University.

Usually, now, we call him Wartuma, which is his name as known among Aboriginal people. He was also known as Charlie Tjaruru Tjungurrayi and Charlie Tarawa Tjungurrayi.[1]

This painting is his "own Dreaming," the ancestral place he was conceived and from which he derives an important component of his identity, and the place he was most identified with—although he painted lots of places—a place called Tjitururrnga, in the Dover Hills. Many mythological stories come together there, but there's also said to be a spirit there, inside a rock formation, that is called out to punish people or to carry out "justice."

3.1 Wartuma (Charlie Tarawa/Tjaruru) Tjungurrayi, *The Trial*, 1972. Synthetic polymer paint on composition board, 76.04 × 40.32 cm. © Estate of the artist | Aboriginal Artists Agency Ltd.

At the same time, the story of Tjitururrnga is also about frost, often called "ice story" or similar names. *Nyinnga* or *kuwarla*, or frost, is one of the features of the place that is involved here. In some documentations of this story, the word *kuwarla* is used interchangeably with *nyinnga*—for frost, ice, or even the mist rising from the ground on cold days.

TS *Icons of the Desert* gives us three descriptions of this painting. There is a summary of Pat Hogan's original notes from 1972 in the 2004 sale catalog, which gives a literal meaning to each element: the central set of circles is a man condemned to death; the pink lines around him are the fingers of the spirits of his dead victims signaling his impending death; the lines of circles along the top and bottom are elders sitting in council; the black lines from them to the central circle are their condemnatory judgment; the three double U-shapes at either side of the central figure are the executioners.[2] In her essay in the *Icons* catalog, Vivien Johnson casts doubt on whether Pintupi justice was dispensed in such a (Western) manner. She thinks that the painting is less about one individual transgressor than (I quote her) "the sentence of death that would be imposed on unlawful intruders to *Wati Kuwarla*'s [Frost Man's] sacred cave at Tjitururrnga."[3]

FM Well, Wartuma had a great ability, using metaphors, to translate between English and Pintupi for people, because he'd had a lot of experience. He worked for the army in Alice Springs in the war. This idea of the "judgment," I think, is a kind of a translation into English or Australian legal vocabulary of a punishing spirit. These are the men who would've come there to raise the spirit against the person that they were going to punish. I guess I would say that Wartuma was trying to communicate with Pat Hogan, who spoke no Pintupi and who had minimal knowledge of Aboriginal culture. Somehow, they found this "mediation," as I might call it, a semi-adequate translation.

TS So, this is a painting about judgment. . . .

FM Punishment. Revenge, punishment, you know, Aboriginal justice in a way.

TS But the ways that this punishment is pictured here implies that it's something that's done by a community. . . .

FM I wouldn't use the word "community" ever in this context. I think that such words communicate a kind of political organization that is more bounded and discrete than Aboriginal social forms. What the painting suggests, I think, is the presence of people who have the authority, based on their relationship to this place, who have the right to make the judgment of wrongdoing or harm and to exercise that right through imposing the punishment. When I visited there, the oldest man came on the trip and gave us a brief but pointed lecture about the rock formation. Only he and the others could call forth the punishing spirit.

TS Okay. What I'm sensing here is that, pictographically, Wartuma has arrived at a way of showing the structure of this process *and*, at the same time, showing it in operation. When I say structure, I mean the basic organization of the elements, the composition. As in most art, it works to establish general resonances while also showing how more specific things fit into the overall picture. One of his basic compositional moves is obvious: symmetry . . . between, in this case, what we see as the upper and lower halves of the overall image—although, of course, that above and below hierarchy does not hold, not least because this was painted horizontally, flat on the ground. The two "halves" are equal, repetitions occurring at the same time, like two hands opening out, palms up.

Anyway, this generates an overall shape that is grounded and bordered at its outer limits by the thick black bands and seems to feed into the center, through the black lines that cut through these densely white-dotted fields, surrounding the central black circle and the figure within it, as if it is locking them in place.

The figure in the middle is striking: a set of concentric circles rendered in pink, seven of them, with armlike tentacles, each of them a double, reaching out to the perimeter of the circle, where the dots curve their ends. The dots always indicate spiritual presence, as we saw so strongly in the Kingsley painting. But around this figure they seem especially intense. The figure seems trapped in the black space, which perhaps evokes the cave, an internal space of some kind. But the figure already possesses enormous energy, or that energy is being poured into it.

FM Well, yes, it looks like it's trapped visually. It's surrounded. The black area seems as if it is an inside.

TS If we took that central figure out for a moment and just looked at it by itself, what do we see?

FM In some of Shorty Lungkarta's paintings, like the *Classic Pintupi Water Dreaming* we just discussed, we also see many such circles, a similar intensity of concentricity. I think part of it is that he [Wartuma] wants the figure to seem bigger, stronger, more intense, and the only way to do that is to do more of them. Perhaps it has to do with the significance of the figure, which would not signify if it were smaller.

So, oddly, my question becomes, Is that central shape the punishing spirit, or is that the punished person? Because Wartuma would tell the story in a more general fashion, such as "This is when we call him out, we do it to punish that person who did wrong. We're gonna get even with him." Unless you asked him exactly "Which one is that?" . . .

TS . . . you wouldn't know.

You are surely right about the key question. Are we to take the central figure as symbolizing the punishment of one transgressive individual, of any one person who transgresses? Or are we seeing the punishment spirit in action?

It could, of course, work on all these registers. As it is in so many ceremonies and paintings. And most storytelling.

FM I'm also interested in these horizontal lines that connect the figures inside the black bands along the top and the bottom. They might have something to do with the way in which he understands the ceremonial practice that was involved there. It's the men [elders, senior people] coming together, the people from there coming together. Interesting, why he has a line crossing through them there. It's very unusual to show people sitting in that way, in that lineup. Maybe they have a hair string that they're holding together, as they do in ceremony, and perhaps the use of that "linkage" is itself signifying their collective identity. You can see a similar thing in William Barak's drawings of ceremonies in Southeast Australia in the late nineteenth century.[4]

I love this painting. I think that the energy for me is that there is something in there that's trapped. The sense of containment, don't you think, is very strong?

And, like Kingsley, he decided to put dots around the outside of the image, at the perimeters, top and bottom, and parts of the sides although not everywhere. Small dots . . .

TS Absolutely. Yes, containment. And struggle against it.

The overall symmetry gives a sense of everything being fixed in time, as powerfully static, but there are so many different kinds of energies at work here that you feel its parts—spirits, people, events, seasons—moving through different kinds of time at this one place.

FM This takes us back to "frost." As I said, ice is strongly identified with this place. So, the fields of white dots might evoke the frost and, through that, cold. Interestingly, in some kinds of body painting, they have black lines rendered in charcoal. For the white effect, bush cotton is stuck to the body. Additionally, body painting sometimes had its own "framing," if I can call it that, with something like what we see in this painting: a bar at the top and one at the bottom, with different shapes inside, as it were. These particular body decorations could easily be transferred to the rectangular shape of the painting support.

Wartuma's composition might also evoke actual features of the place too. There are many different ancestral lines that go through Tjitururrnga. The avenging spirit we have been mentioning is said to be there. And they call it forth. I don't know how it's related to all the other ones there. There are sev-

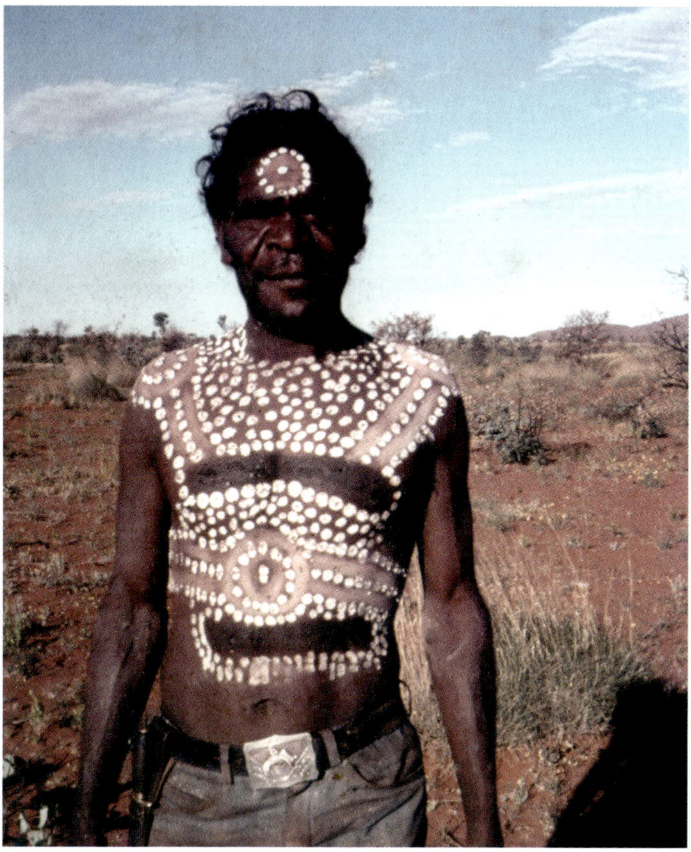

3.2 Allen Tjapanangka painted for a ceremony, Alumbra Bore, Northern Territory, 1970. Photograph by Terry Parry. Used with permission of living male relatives, Matthew Pinta Tjapangarti and Bobby West Tjupurrula.

eral different geological formations. There's a creek that runs off. And a big rock hole that's identified with an ancestral Dreaming: the golden bandicoot [*mingatjurru*] comes by there and hides his fire stick up his rectum, refusing to share it with the two rabbit-eared bandicoots [*ninu* or bilby] who are traveling with him. As they try to go on, the *ninu* die from the cold and go into the ground. No doubt, there is more meaning there than I can catch. The area is also very rich in yams. People would dig them there.

Wartuma was enormously proud of his connection and painted this place often, usually with expansive white fields of this kind, and in many more ways than we can easily survey here.

TS Years ago, I was very struck by a painting of his in the Art Gallery of New South Wales, done in 1989, which they label *Wati G'wala* or *Iceman Dreaming*. I recall that the caption invited us to think of it as evoking ancestral memories of the Ice Age, through which Indigenous people lived. This is an astonishing time scale.

FM I think this is fanciful, tricked-up fabulation. The white sheens are about frost in the desert, the occurrence of ice, not the Ice Age.

TS There are several similarities between the painting we are discussing and another in the Wilkerson collection, also painted in 1989, which is just as challenging to those looking for settled interpretations. It is an important work and is also of a good size, about four feet square. It has the intriguing title *Audience with the Queen*.

Like *The Trial*, we have two quite different interpretations noted in the *Icons* catalog. The certificate written by the then art advisor Daphne Williams, based on talking to the artist, suggests that the central roundel is Buckingham Palace, or a room inside the palace where he met the queen; the faint white roundels are her, him, and others in the room; the straight white lines around the border are the palace guards. In total contrast, Vivien Johnson and Roger Benjamin favor a deeper level, on which this is "the home of the redoubtable Ice Man in his freezing cave, Wati Kuwarla."[5]

To me, Wartuma's paintings invite us into a zone of thought and feeling that parallels Melville's famous riff, in *Moby-Dick*, on the incessant incantation of whiteness. He says that it is the most meaningful symbol of the spiritual *and* of mankind's most appalling aspects. He also, if I remember, evokes snow, wild landscapes, saying that what he calls their dumb blankness is

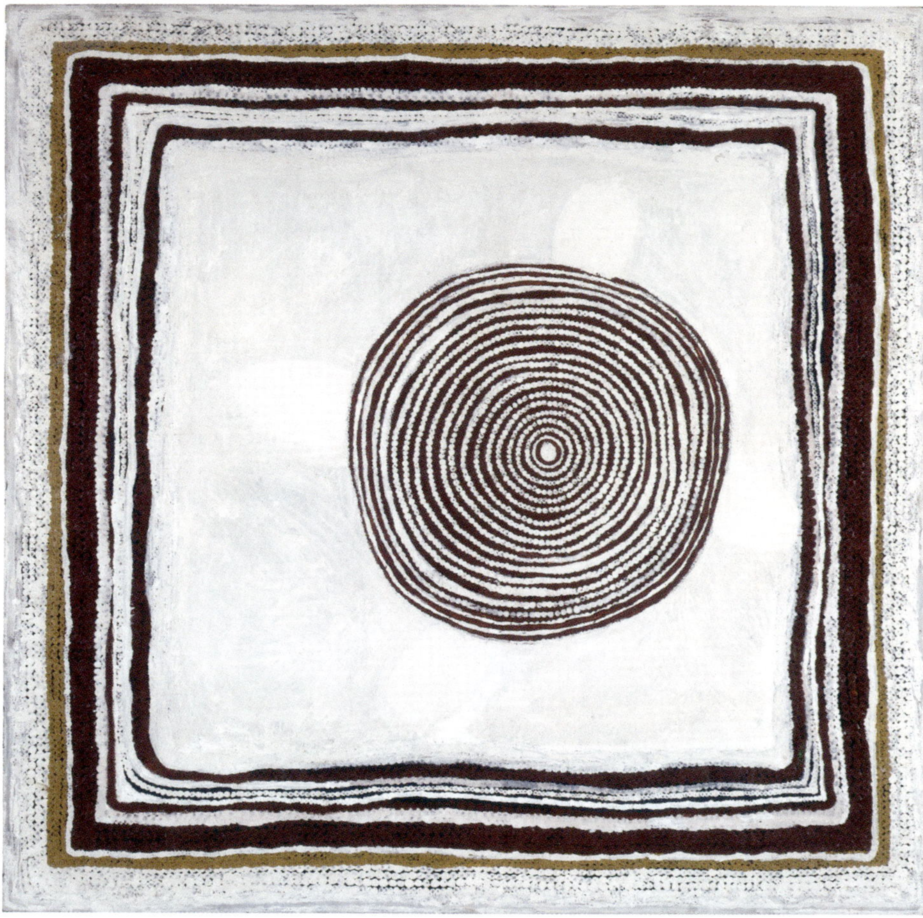

3.3 Wartuma (Charlie Tarawa/Tjaruru) Tjungurrayi, *Audience with the Queen*, 1989. Synthetic polymer paint on linen, 120.02 × 120.33 cm. © Estate of the artist | Aboriginal Artists Agency Ltd.

full of meaning.[6] Today, Blackness needs just as much, even more urgent, explaining.

FM Personally, I favor the view that this "audience with the queen" belongs with our understanding of *The Trial*, with the central concentric roundel enclosed within the larger field, as if trapped inside . . . a cave.

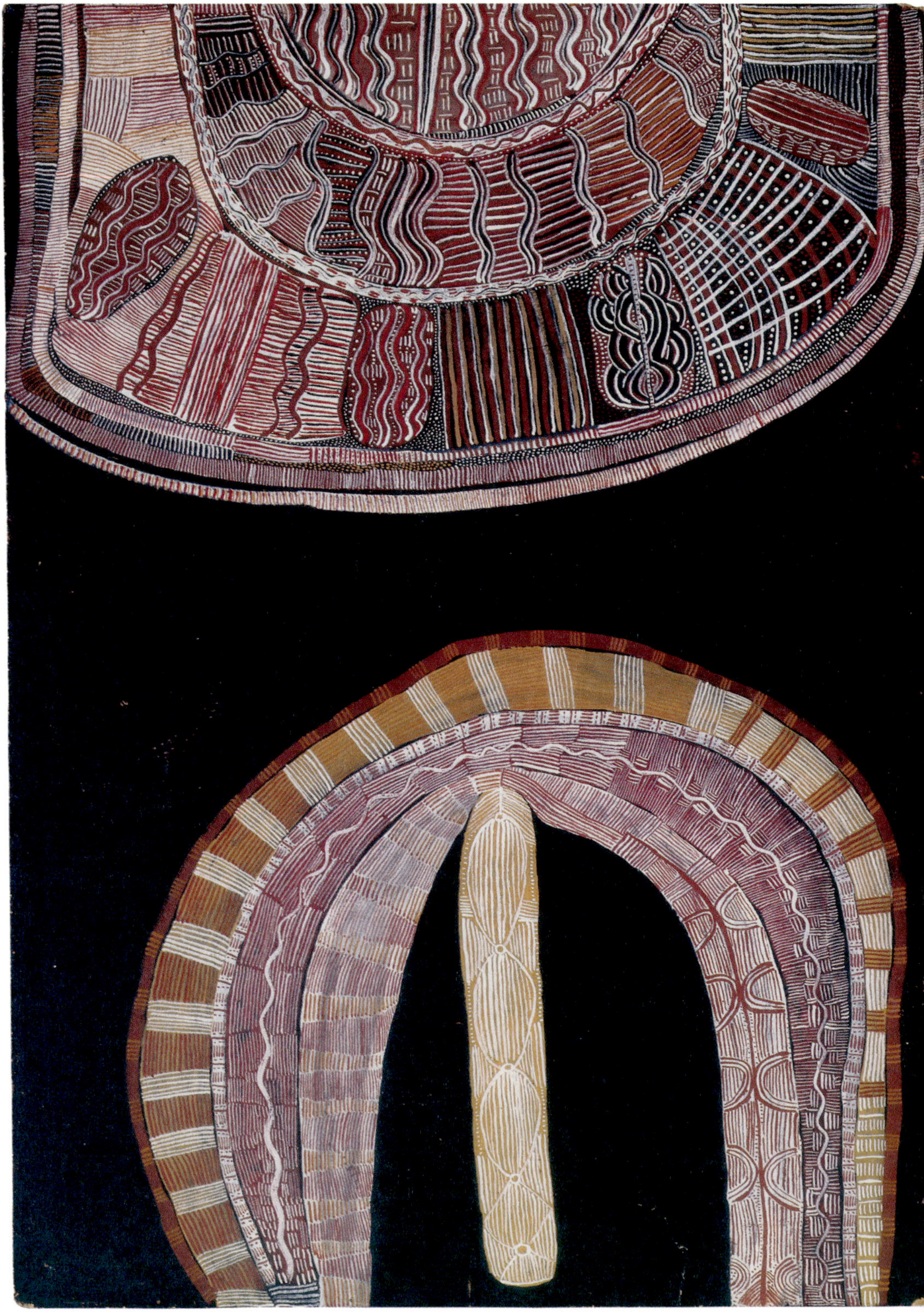

4 INSIDE AND OUTSIDE

A Cave Allegory

Mick Namarari Tjapaltjarri, *Big Cave Dreaming with Ceremonial Objects*, 1972

TS Let's go to a painting that is unequivocally about a cave. Mick Namarari Tjapaltjarri's *Big Cave Dreaming with Ceremonial Objects*, made, we are told, in late 1972.

FM Yes, he was quite an interesting man, very quiet and self-contained, speaking in very low tones. He was a Pintupi/Luritja man, identified principally with a place called Marnpi, which is at the eastern edge of Pintupi/Luritja country. He was very closely related to Benny Tjapaltjarri, who's the subject of the film *Benny and the Dreamers*, and Namarari appears in that film.[1] In 1978, Bardon made a short experimental film about Namarari, *Mick and the Moon*. Namarari also has custodial rights to Mitukatjirri, which is an important *Tingarri* place. And it really is a cave.

I believe that this painting is about Mitukatjirri because it was done in 1972, possibly not long after Roger Sandall and Jeremy Long took Pintupi

4.1 Mick Namarari Tjapaltjarri, *Big Cave Dreaming with Ceremonial Objects*, 1972. Synthetic polymer powder paint on composition board, 91.2 × 63.82 cm. © Estate of the artist | Aboriginal Artists Agency Ltd.

men for their third trip to reenact a ritual in their own country so that it could be filmed. The first two visits were to the sacred sites of Yumari and Yaru Yaru.[2] The third film was to be called *Pintupi Revisit Mitukatjirri*. Many men were involved. They were very attentive to it. But in the end, people complained about the filming and payment, so it was never edited and completed. The footage is still at the Institute for Aboriginal Studies in Canberra. Access is restricted.

This cave, Mitukatjirri, holds an important story, thus the word "big" in the title. It is related to the *Tingarri* cycle of Dreaming stories, in this case one traveling from the Docker River area [Kaltukatjarra] up through the Kintore Range. It's also painted by the famous artist Turkey Tolson Tjupurrula, whose father was a principal custodian. Turkey and Namarari were very close, part of the same family. Another important place is nearby: Ilingawurrngawurrnga, which was painted by Shorty Lungkarta in 1974 on canvas.

TS Is it the one that is made up of several constellations of concentric circles, most of which are overlapping each other? This generates an extraordinary three-dimensionality, a layering, as if these brightly colored discs were spinning in space. It takes some looking to see the mapping lines underneath and to realize that the spinning stacks that seem to hover above that background do actually follow travel storylines up the left side and the center as we look at it. We are so used to seeing them inscribed flat to the surface.

Again, such inventiveness during these early years. You trace the evolution of Shorty's style in your essay in the *Icons* book.[3]

FM Yes, I do. By the way, this same place is also the subject of Turkey Tolson's famous series of *Straightening Spears* paintings. Mitukatjirri is a big gathering place where the ancestral *Tingarri* men got together for ceremony. It was a major source of inspiration to these men. It was a big deal to go back there in 1972 after so many years away, a return from the exile they were experiencing. It's one of the most important *Tingarri* sites along the way, on their path coming from Docker River, right up toward Kintore and then on from there.

At these ceremonies, a (ceremonial) pole is erected, a distinctive feature of numerous desert men's ceremonies. I once saw the film footage of it. It is wound around with grass and so on to flesh it out and then bound with hair string—fiber made from human hair. Then it's decorated with vegetable down, paint, and so on, similar to body decoration. In this case, I remember seeing one of the young initiates climb the pole. I think that this oblong feature here in the bottom part, in black space, is the pole, what I will call the

Tingarri pole.[4] That was a big, prominent part of the ceremony. Similar ceremonial poles were documented photographically by the early anthropological witnesses, notably Baldwin Spencer and Francis Gillen in 1899, but they are considered too sacred to show publicly now in explicit form.[5] They were represented in somewhat generic form in cover illustrations for the early exhibitions of Albert Namatjira, the Arrernte artist, who himself did not record such restricted images in his own work.[6] The presence in these paintings is only suggested rather than fully represented.

According to the annotations about this painting by Bardon and others, the upper form in the painting is a cliff edge, with water running off the cliffs. I am guessing this is a place called Ligertwood Cliffs or near that spot. These geological features are being viewed from above.

So, if I am right, we have two images: one, an outside, seen from above, and another, an inside, seen from inside out.

It has fascinated me for a long time how people who don't have a tradition of representation of depth work out such ingenious ways to communicate such interior space within the limitations and possibilities of painting. I am also amazed by how rarely this is discussed by the interpreters of this art.

TS Let's do that right now.

FM Well, in this painting, within the upper, semicircular form that suggests, by inference really, the cliff edges, there are four quite conventional icons—the elliptical shapes with designs on them that look like decorated shields.

TS Bardon labels them *tjurungas*. They seem to be large, important ones.

FM The designs and shape indicate, to me, these sorts of carved and decorated (usually wooden) oblong objects but they may also be shields, often decorated for ceremonies. The word *tjurunga* or *churinga* [there are various orthographies, now usually written as *twyerrenge*] refers very broadly to what we could call ceremonial objects, although there are many specific, individually delineated types and sizes of these objects.

TS It reminds me somewhat of what Tim Leura Tjapaltjarri did in his *Spirit Dreaming through Napperby Country* painting of 1980, you know, the sequence of major Dreaming stories, rendered as separate *tjurungas*, or as sand paintings, or as see-through holes ("windows") into other spaces or dimensions, strung along a journey line between several places. Not around the side of a cliff face, as it is here, but across a long stretch of country. We know that Bardon commissioned it to use in a film about Tim Leura's life that he was making. I have always wondered whether he asked for it to be panoramic so that he could film it and presumably edit in relevant imagery as the camera pans across it. Certainly, Bardon's reading of it is highly emotional. As if it were the artist's last testament.[7]

FM Namarari's painting has a very different focus. It is on the Dreaming place itself. These shieldlike shapes sit on the same surface as the wavy lines indicating the cliffs and the running water, which are presented with equal force and precision of detail.

TS Bardon labels the thin band around the perimeter of the upper shape "cliffs," and the band around the bottom shape "rocks and strata." To me, these are simply necessary to define the edges, to distinguish the shapes from the black void, which Bardon labels "night."

FM The Pintupi word for night is *munga*, which also refers to darkness. . . .

TS Certainly, many important ceremonies do take place at night. Perhaps the ceremony associated with the cave below does take place then. Compositionally, however, Namarari needs the black space for the spatial reversal between the two shapes to occur. In other words, for us to get the point that the cave (below) is actually located inside these cliffs (above).

FM Looking at the bottom part of the painting, we see this very strong shape, with many specifics inside it. The inner band on the right includes the semicircles of some men sitting, perhaps singing ceremonies. There are eight or ten of them, yet they're facing away from each other. Frankly, I don't know if this is significant, but typically, in ceremonies, the men who are not performing themselves gather around to sing the performers into action, the very songs the ancestral figures themselves sang as they enacted their presence.

These figures do not appear on the other side. There is asymmetry within the overall symmetry of this shape, as there is in the shape above.

The wavy white line coursing through the next band, the inner arc, could be a hair string. Bardon's annotation says it is water going in a fissure in the rock, but it is possible that this feature is represented in ritual as a hair string carried or deployed by the *Tingarri* men, now marked as this feature in the rock.

TS If we track it from the right side, that wavy line begins with little vertical marks as if they are footprints, but there are too many to indicate an animal dreaming. Maybe they indicate water seeping through the rock into the cave. They dissipate, mostly disappear as the line weaves around the top to the other side, but not entirely. Lots of stippling throughout this painting . . .

FM In his dissertation, John Kean has some insights that can help us here. He is very attentive to the artistic or painterly interaction between Namarari and Tim Leura at this time—and between them and Kaapa Tjampitjinpa. He argues that they were trying to figure out together what it was that they were painting. A ceremony? Or the place?[8] They seem to have arrived at a conception in which the place incorporates the ceremony. Indeed, the ceremony represents the ancestral action at the place that left the features of the place as one sees them now. In a sense they are the same, or perhaps two sides of the same coin? That seems to be going on here as well, an effort to blend these two tasks into one that can be seen at once, that is, as a configuration.

TS Right. As we have been saying, some of the imagery is conventional, a matter of reproducing certain given sacred designs, known for millennia, immediately readable. But other forms are obviously being discovered, or uncovered, disclosed might say it better, in the process of making a specific painting.

For example, it is natural for us experienced viewers of cropped photographs and representational paintings to assume that a shape like the one at the top of this painting is the presently visible section of a form that begins outside, well above the top edge of the painting. A rock formation of whatever size it is . . . we see the part we see and assume the rest is roughly similar. Here, the place is implied as extending way beyond the top of the picture frame.

The bottom shape seems more complete, perhaps . . . but, actually, it is hard to read as an overall gestalt. We can see that it is a cave, but where are we standing to look? Inside the cave, it seems, its walls wrapping around us, seeing what is happening to the walls, what happened in the Dreaming, and what occurs inside the space of the cave.

As you said before, we have a mixture of a three-dimensional view from above at the top and a three-dimensional view from inside below that does not look into a distance, look out, for instance. This is adding up to a distinctive kind of two-dimensionality. . . .

I also see a kind of magnetism between the two main forms, triggered not only by the black field between them, but by the push upward of the *tjurunga* or, as you prefer, pole as it penetrates the arc at the top of the cave. It is incredibly phallic, raising the question of the gender of the cave itself. And of the huge force of the shape above pressing down toward the shape below . . .

FM There's a lot of Aboriginal imagery that is almost unconscious, much that is not necessarily commented on. Including such combinations of male and female matters. That's what Géza Róheim, a psychoanalytically trained anthropologist of the mid-twentieth century, was always so interested in.[9] He saw *churingas* or *tjurungas*, which had circles on them, as being a kind of endless repetition of that combination. And the men—of course, the phallic nature of poles decorated and erected for male ceremony is not lost on them. Namarari does that in a lot of his paintings. These levels of meaning are interwoven, like a knot, you know what I mean?

I know that Bardon indicated this feature as a *tjurunga*, which many people would understand as an oval, wood-carved sacred object. But having seen and heard about this and other *Tingarri* ceremonies, and this one in particular, the reference to a sacred object as heard by Bardon could very likely be to this, another specific form of *tjurunga*, known by words with which Bardon would be unfamiliar. Reaching for equivalents that might be familiar to non-Aboriginal people, Wartuma Tjungurrayi once told me such poles worked like "the wireless" [radio broadcasting], like "telegraph poles," he said. Indeed, the word *tjurunga* has a wider application than just any one form.

TS One more thing about the composition of this painting. In most paintings from Papunya, indeed most paintings by Aboriginal artists, there's an integration of all the elements of the story into one configuration, visually: thus the use of symmetry as a kind of norm within which variation can be indicated. Here, however, we've got two views on this one story. The configuration is as if a division like that between heaven and hell is being shown.

FM Well, you know, there is the visible and the hidden, always. There is what's *yuti* [visible, sensibly present]: everybody can see it. And there is *Tjukurrpa* [Dreaming], the inside, the restricted.[10]

TS I'm just trying to make a point about just how radical the visualization of the whole is here.

FM Yes. He's a very inventive artist. Around this time, he did another painting of the same subject, with a similar lower section, except that the interior of the cave is fully painted and the *tjurunga* inside it lies horizontally. The upper half shows three Dreaming areas divided into sections, the lower one touching the top of the cave.[11]

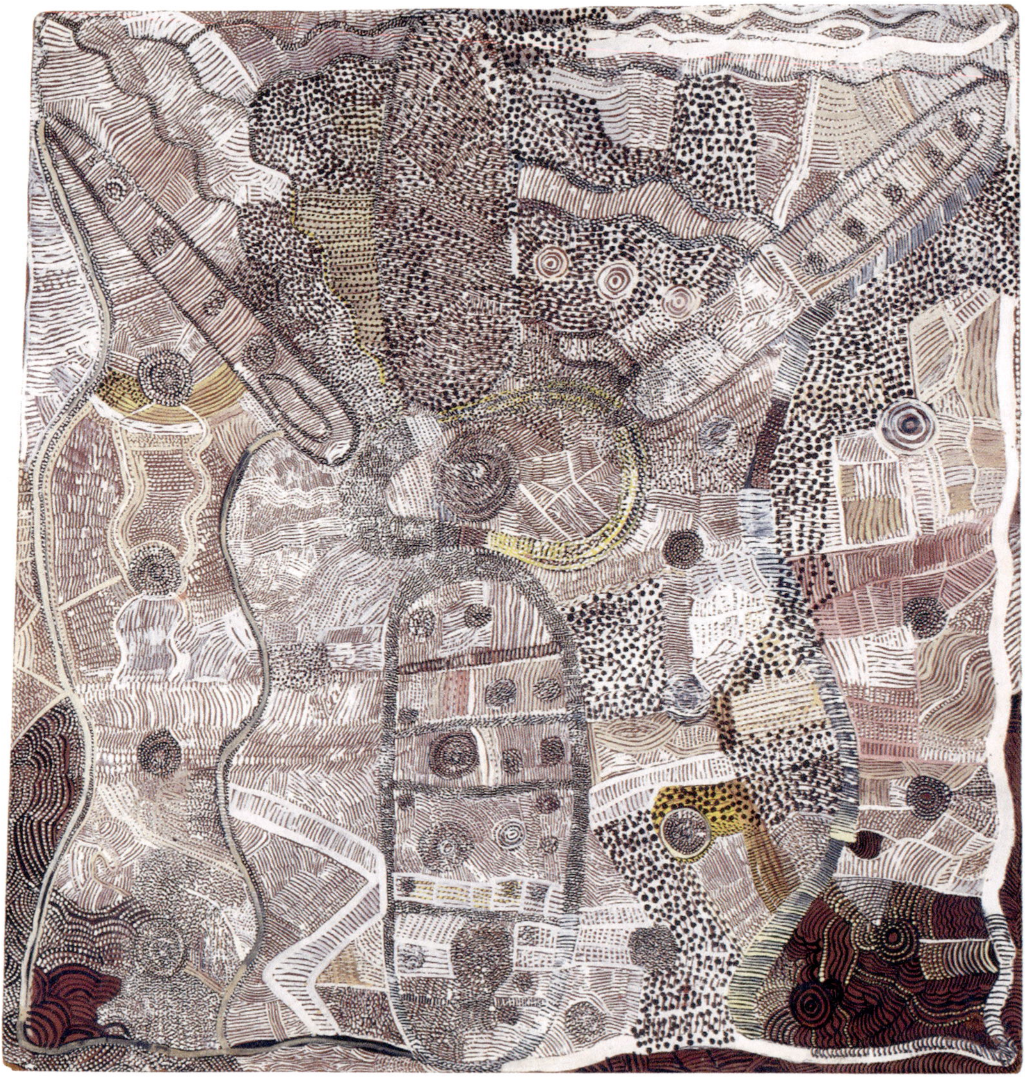

5.1 Johnny Warangkula Tjupurrula, *Water Dreaming at Kalipinypa*, August 1972. Synthetic polymer on composition board, 80.65 × 75.57 cm. © Estate of the artist | Aboriginal Artists Agency Ltd.

5 STIPPLING PLENITUDE

"The Water Man Does Not Get Wet —He Is the Rain Itself"

Johnny Warangkula Tjupurrula, *Water Dreaming at Kalipinypa*, 1972

TS Johnny Warangkula Tjupurrula's *Water Dreaming at Kalipinypa* is emerging as the masterpiece among these early paintings done at Papunya. So much has been said about this picture, and well said, by so many. In the *Icons of the Desert* catalog, Roger Benjamin says, "The visual fascination of this, the greatest picture in the exhibition, lies in the delicacy of the artist's veiling of things and in the way the site at Kalipinypa is divided into dozens of small compartments, no two of which are the same."[1] What can we add?

Perhaps we could explore the idea and practice of "veiling" a little more. Of course, it is pivotal to the second phase of painting at Papunya, the obligatory shift away from straightforward presentations of sacred ceremonial icons in the manner most rapidly developed in the early months by Kaapa Mbitjana Tjampitjinpa. You can see some examples of "School of Kaapa" paintings in the background of the color photographs taken in late August 1972 by the photojournalist Michael Jensen, of the group working in the shed on several paintings, including this one. The earlier works lean against the bench or are propped on it, as if they were references for the artists—or perhaps Bardon just put them there to increase the information in the photographs.

As we know, the depiction of sacred icons and of ceremonial figures on objects that were being circulated among the uninitiated caused consternation in nearby communities, not least at Yuendumu, and in Alice Springs. All-over dotting quickly emerged as the preferred way of honoring that sacred content and spreading its effects while at the same time, and in the same painterly gesture, keeping it secret. It takes a device already used for announcing the presence of the sacred and generalizes it across the whole surface, turning it into a screen, one that reveals and conceals at the same time.

Does this doubling between concealing and revealing—a kind of *unconcealing*, as Heidegger would have it—happen for the first time in this painting? Hard to know, as several of the artists working in the same space

5.2 The Men's Painting Room, Papunya, August 1972. *From left:* Yala Yala Gibbs Tjungurrayi, Wartuma (Charlie Tarawa/Tjaruru)) Tjungurrayi, Timmy Payungka Tjapangarti, Kaapa Mbitjana Tjampitjinpa, Johnny Warangkula Tjupurrula, and Old Walter Tjampitjinpa. Photograph by Michael Jensen.

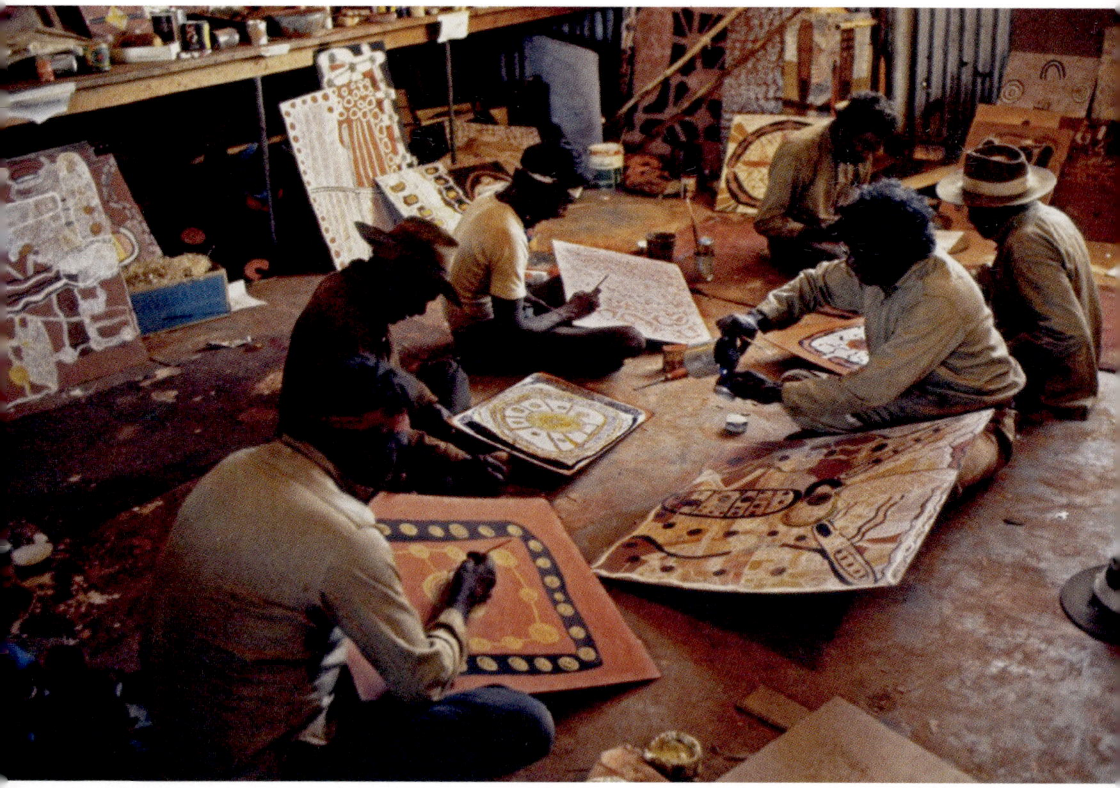

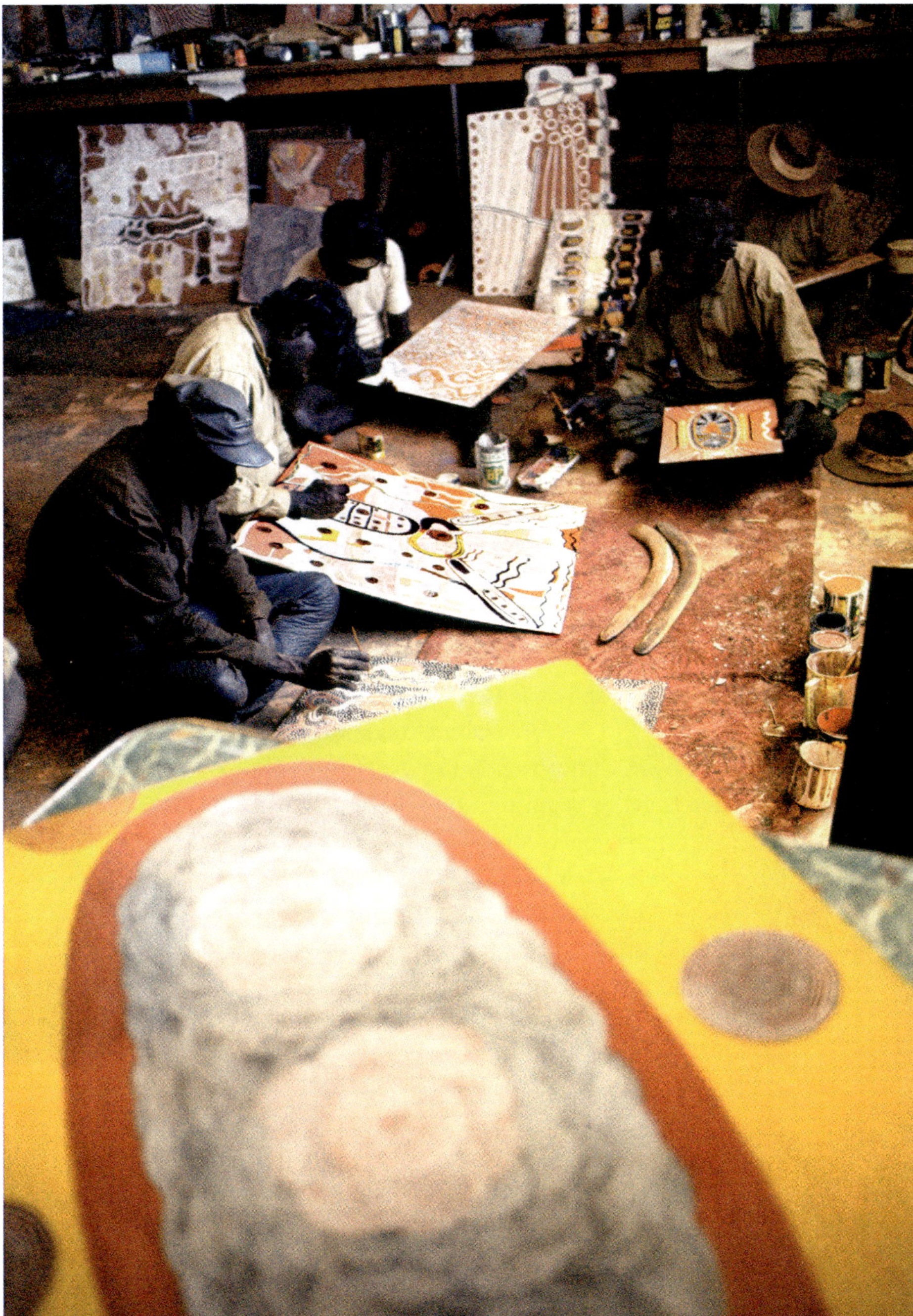

5.3 The Men's Painting Room, Papunya, August 1972. *From left:* Wartuma (Charlie Tarawa/ Tjaruru) Tjungurrayi, Johnny Warangkula Tjupurrula, Timmy Payungka Tjapangarti, Kaapa Mbitjana Tjampitjinpa, and Old Walter Tjampitjinpa. Photograph by Michael Jensen.

during these months began to foreground dotting. It might simply be that Warangkula, along with Walter Tjampitjinpa, had a major responsibility for the Water Dreaming, which conventionally calls up lots of white dots, splashes, blurry white patches. Another of the photographs shows Walter painting a Rainbow and Water Dreaming picture right next to him. And, as we know, it poured with rain at Papunya during this time. There were floods.

If we look closely at the Jensen photograph (fig. I.2) where four of the painters sit on the ground and another four (actually five, Kaapa is hiding behind his painting) stand behind them, posing awkwardly—Warangkula has *Water Dreaming at Kalipinypa* propped on a table, upside-down from how we usually see it now—we can see that Shorty Lungkarta is close to finishing the dotting in his *Classic Pintupi Water Dreaming*. Clifford Possum, in the foreground, is only partway through *Honey Ant Ceremony*—the one now in the Art Gallery of South Australia—but he has already completed the amazing central section, where the three main symbols inside the ceremonial space are conceived as clustered concentric discs, in four layers, like unfolding flowers. These rosettes sit on top of clouds of black-on-white discs that are themselves stacked in many layers. This is an extraordinarily resonant field, swirling inside itself.

Another photograph by Jensen (fig. 5.3) shows the blurred edge of Clifford Possum's painting in the foreground. It is almost as if we were looking at the other artists from Clifford's point of view! Both photos reveal that Johnny Warangkula is yet to begin the stippling that will lift his design to another dimension. But his basic composition is already more complex than what Clifford Possum is attempting, on this occasion at least. *Water Dreaming at Kalipinypa* will soon become, arguably, the most subtle of the "veiled" works made then and since.

I love Kean's celebration of Warangkula as "the inventor of the articulate dot."[2] That is so apt for many of his paintings from this time and afterward. Yet as we look at this painting, bearing in mind the subsequent, almost universal adoption of dotting, mostly white dotting, by artists throughout the region, I am struck by the almost total absence of white dots in it.

They are there, but only inside a few roundels indicating sacred places, in some of the bands on the left side, and as indicators of rows in the bottom left and right sections, the least developed areas. What does most of the work in this painting is the incredibly delicate, very small, in fact, tiny in most cases, white brushstrokes, made with a watercolor brush. They move in multiple different directions, and every stroke is *inside* the configurations that they're meant—according to the general idea—to be obscuring. Clearly, as we look at this painting, these marks are doing the opposite. Each white stroke is working with a set of similar ones to *bring out* the character of the area that they are delineating. It's a kind of stippling, the engraving technique, also used a lot in illustrative drawing in the European tradition. What is astonishing here is its variety. And its use across such a wide range of colors, most similar in hue.

To me, this is a touch that is not unlike some of the best painting on bark, that of John Mawurndjul, for example, where the crosshatching of tiny strokes [*rarrk*] works in similar ways.[3]

FM Yes, there are very few white dots. Yet it does feel as if you're looking a bit through a veil of some kind. If you take up Howard Morphy's argument about the importance of the "shimmer effect" in Aboriginal art generally, this one really does dazzle the eyes.[4]

TS So, the cumulative effect—a kind of gentle agitation, and the sense of everything growing, thriving, even though it is not done through white dots—is certainly achieved through the stippling, the preponderance of tiny white strokes.

In this case at least, any "obscuring" of sacred content—if obscuring or veiling is what it is—occurs as a secondary effect of this dense but low-key dazzling.

FM This is a crucially important point. I think that the breakthrough we are talking about was the result of a few very inventive artists working alongside each other, striving to solve the problem of how to get their stories out, using these relatively unfamiliar materials, on these prepared boards. Tim Leura and Kaapa Tjampitjinpa, and some Anmatyerr painters, were right there, and Warangkula was very much sitting next to them.

In terms of the stories they wanted to share, the key problem, as many commentators have said, is whether to do so by painting the ceremony relating to a place or painting the place itself. This is Kean's argument. Kaapa and others had made an impression by painting the elements of important ceremonies—the *churingas*, other sacred items, ground markings, poles, ancestor animals, figures that could either be the ancestor or a person performing a *corroboree*, and so on. A notorious example, Clifford Possum Tjapaltjarri's *Emu Corroboree Man*, from early 1972, is also in this collection.[5] But if you can't any longer do this so overtly, then painting the place, using the signs for it, is a good option. Such signs are already abstract, but they can be made specific.

This painting's not about a ceremony. It's about a place; it is what its title says: *Water Dreaming at Kalipinypa*. John Kean makes a convincing case, as does Dick Kimber, that it is primarily the story of Winpa, the Lightning Man, bringing a storm there.[6] The painting shows its effects on the land. Warangkula painted this subject very often. He was very attached to it.

The ancestral man Winpa sings out from inside the cave, which is shown at the center of this painting. I have been there. It's not a deep cave, more a rock hole within a bigger claypan, where water accumulates. I have heard it said that the iron content of the soil there attracts lightning strikes.

To me, Dick Kimber was the great discussant of what was actually *in* this painting. He knew Warangkula well, had been out to this country with people. He emphasized that the painting really draws attention to the richness and fertility of the place and the plant life around it, which I think is more marked in this than a lot of other earlier paintings. The black dotting in the upper portion, for instance, is identified as *kampurarrpa*—black bush currant (or bush raisin)—that grows in this area after the rains.

My guess is that the oval *churinga*-like objects that are overpainted, and thus sort of suppressed by virtue of the filling in of so much of their interior space, might be actions of ancestors, the land shapes formed by them—what we see as geological and geographical features. They're represented in the forms that they might have had in the ancestral realm and the Dreaming, left behind by these ancestors—a *churinga* or another sacred object that turns to a sandhill, or that moves up a sandhill. So, Warangkula's bringing together the actual vegetation after rains, the country springing to life, all of which is caused by this ancestral activity. That's the source of it. Right? So, I would say, rather than them being covered, they're *embedded* in this landscape—which is, of course, always already ancestral.

I'm reminded of a painting by the Arnhem Land artist David Malangi about Murayana, an ancestral figure who is shown lying on the ground, with plants growing out of his body. As if he is one with the land.[7] So, Warangkula's technique, like Malangi, allows you to sense that these features, in their ancestral form, are there.

TS I love your explanation of why those *churingas* are all converging as if magnetically drawn to this one place. You are saying that those spirits and their great stories over the millennia are connected and converge on this place for him. And that they figure actual geological formations . . .

FM They *could* do so, they *might*.... I can't be sure. I never spoke with Warangkula or other custodians in any depth about this place, but even if I had done so, the levels of knowledge and specificity would have been more than I could comprehend.

Let's look more closely at the specific features. I think Bardon himself noticed that on the left, running up and down vertically, there is a kind of structure: three concentric circles that are connected by two sets of wavy lines. He identifies them as a water symbol or a symbol that's used as a conventional icon for Water Dreaming, for traveling between waterholes.

TS It is framed in a way by the two wavy lines that descend from the upper left *churinga*.

FM You are suggesting that these are objects that men use to call forth the power of the ceremony. Okay. The sounds they make are probably connected to the activities of the Rain Dreaming.

TS Pretty close to the center of the painting is a roundel with many concentric circles in it that seems to be the pivot of the whole composition. To its left is a curved, "sitting-down" shape, a big black one that stands out in the photographs of this board when he was outlining the main stories but now is scarcely visible. On the other side of the roundel is a striking, sweeping curve, marked in yellow, wrapping around the central circle.

I am reminded of a quotation that Bardon includes in his catalog, as he begins his discussion of Warangkula's Water Dreaming paintings. I have it here: "The Water Man does not get wet—he is the rain itself. At night people can see his fire in his cave on the mountains."[8] He doesn't give a source. Perhaps he heard it often, from many of the men. Perhaps it is a line from a song that Warangkula would sing while painting. Whatever, it is a wonderful evocation of presence in absence, of nearness and distance, of things taking different forms simultaneously—and recurrently, over long durations.

So poetically realized in this painting, where the curved figures and the central roundel are scarcely discernible among the arrays of stipples.

FM Looking at some of the paintings of Kalipinypa that have more explicit figures, we can infer that, in this painting, one curve is the Lightning Man sitting, the other is the cave, and the roundel is his fire inside the cave. In other paintings, Warangkula includes a naturalistic representation of the Winpa man himself.[9] People who knew Warangkula well say that sometimes when he was painting, he would take up his boomerangs and sing this story. They are there on the floor in front of him as he paints. He *is* that man, taking on that persona, this story.

These stories travel all the way to Mikanji and other places where people like Kaapa painted, Mikanji being the site and story of the painting Kaapa did that won the Caltex Prize for painting in Alice Springs in 1971. You can imagine how this singing of adjacent and overlapping territories would connect the artists with each other as they painted.

This is speculation. What we can see as we look at the painting are the features that his memory attributes to this place.

TS That's a powerful point you make about them singing together as they paint, sharing the territories from which, being in Papunya, they are estranged.

FM I noticed this about the women's paintings from Papunya that come much later, in the 1980s. There's a kind of blurring of the ancestral past with the present. The paintings are all about the Bush Tucker [the wild food that people gather] that's left behind in the Dreaming by the ancestors, but it's also the place of current activities, of getting bush food today. There's a kind of doubling of the experienced world and its underlying truth, the doubling that I mentioned earlier.[10]

TS This sense is incredibly vivid. Ancient yet amazingly fresh. As if the layering of time was happening physically, in the landscape itself . . .

FM Look at the detail, the many movements in the various parts of the painting. I mean, he's just a very different kind of painter than Tim Leura or the others. Their paintings seem more conceptual and his more action. He's really feeling it.

TS How would you compare it to other many-storied paintings such as Clifford Possum Tjapaltjarri's "map" paintings, the first of which was made at Papunya soon after in 1973, the one called *Paths of the Ancestors*? Or Michael Nelson Jagamara's famous *Five Dreamings*, made much later, in 1984?

FM Well, they painted a series of stories that they had rights to over a broad geographical landscape. This painting, in contrast, is about *one place* and the variety of features connected to it. Of course, the ancestor figures evoked do travel to other places, but that is not the focus of this painting, whereas it was for these artists in those paintings.

TS I am still thinking about the interplay in this painting between three elements: the incredible variety within each of the small sections and between each section when you compare them with each other; the magnetism between the larger elements; and, of course, the white sheen that suffuses the whole. This is fabulous artistic inventiveness, as we say, of finding new form inside a conjunction between known forms and that which is, up to this point, formless.

We celebrate this painting now, precisely because of its deft negotiation of so many contraries. But I remember that Bardon was equivocal about it. I mean, he loved Johnny Warangkula and valorized his art. In the "Selected Catalogue," he accords him first place in the first of his categories: Water Dreaming paintings. He celebrates a now-lost version of this subject in exactly the terms we would use today for *this* painting but says that its intricacies have made it ghostlike, the Water Man spectral, the forms vague. He attributes this to the artist failing to calibrate his passionate drive to share the excitement of his subject with the constraints required by its secret, sacred nature.[11]

Certainly, as we are seeing, this painting goes way beyond the simple match of design and story that Bardon sought, but which the painters often overrode.

FM Well, in terms of coherence, think of the rain rushing over most of what we see, not only the rocky areas toward the center but also the sandhills nearby, reviving the whole landscape . . . the fruit flourishing and growing. To me, the main subject of this painting is plenitude. What the land, with all its history, has afforded, and does so now.

In terms of composition, the magnetism you mention, look how he draws on the diagonals that some of the other painters were trialing at the time. Like the painting in the collection by Long Jack Phillipus Tjakamarra called *Big Family Kangaroo Ceremonial Dreaming*, made in the latter months of 1971.[12]

TS Yes, indeed. If one compares these two paintings, the point you made before about the difference between paintings that are about ceremonies and those that are about place becomes clear. Like several other artists at the time, Long Jack Phillipus depicted ceremonial objects and spirits and people moving to converge on a center for the ceremony. He showed them against a totally black background, perhaps signifying night. Viewers would need to be told what the place is. We cannot see it or sense anything about it. This is a classic "School of Kaapa" painting.

The contrast to Warangkula, in this regard, could not be greater. If he is evoking ceremony in the three main shapes and elsewhere in the painting, he is showing that it emerges—we would say "organically"—from this place. The ancestors were the first performers. "Past and present together" is part of the title of another painting of Kalipinypa he did at this time.[13]

His use of diagonals is as subtle as everything else he does. They do not depend from each of the four corners. The ones from the two top corners suggest a kind of symmetry in the upper half, but not exactly, because the two shapes are different. These shapes make us look for repetitions in the lower half, but each quadrant is structured around a distinct spatial logic: the upper ones are dominated by the two diagonal shapes; on the lower left, there is the up and down of the Water Dreaming travel story; on the lower right, we are given a patchwork of movement and stillness that absorbs the diagonal thrust from above. This right side is dominated, structurally, by the two sets of dots—six and five—that run down through it. No wavy travel lines connect them but there is a long snake or riverlike form wending its way down from the top righthand corner, perhaps from the *churinga* there. This implies some movement across country, although probably only country around this place.

Again, all these elements were very prominent in his under drawing, as we can see in the photographs, yet now they resonate like echoes.

In contrast, there are other devices that constrain the dynamism somewhat. Like Kingsley Tjungurrayi, he has felt the need to delineate the outer edges by indicating a frame of some kind just inside them, at least for most of the painting. These wavy lines are rather tentatively done. It is unclear what they signify. And at the bottom right and left, there are some patches where he has just begun with the first black lines, exposing the brown of the particleboard he is painting on.

FM Perhaps he had run out of energy there, or felt that he had done enough . . . or it might have been picked up for transport to Alice Springs at that moment.

TS Very likely. Thinking of the mood of the whole painting, we have this powerful structure given by the three large shapes pivoting around the central waterhole, and all the other features we have been noticing. But everything is done with a delicate touch. These incredibly tiny strokes, we sense how long it took to do them, which slows down our own time of looking. Turkey Tolson Tjupurrula's dotting comes to mind here as a parallel practice.

FM To me, Warangkula has a much more developed sense of dynamic balance than some of the other earlier painters. I think that's more typical of some of the Pintupi painters, in contrast to Anmatyerr men such as Kaapa, Clifford Possum, and Tim Leura: this finding a form out of a bunch of elements that are being pulled together for the first time, as you say, discovering a way of doing so in the process of doing it.

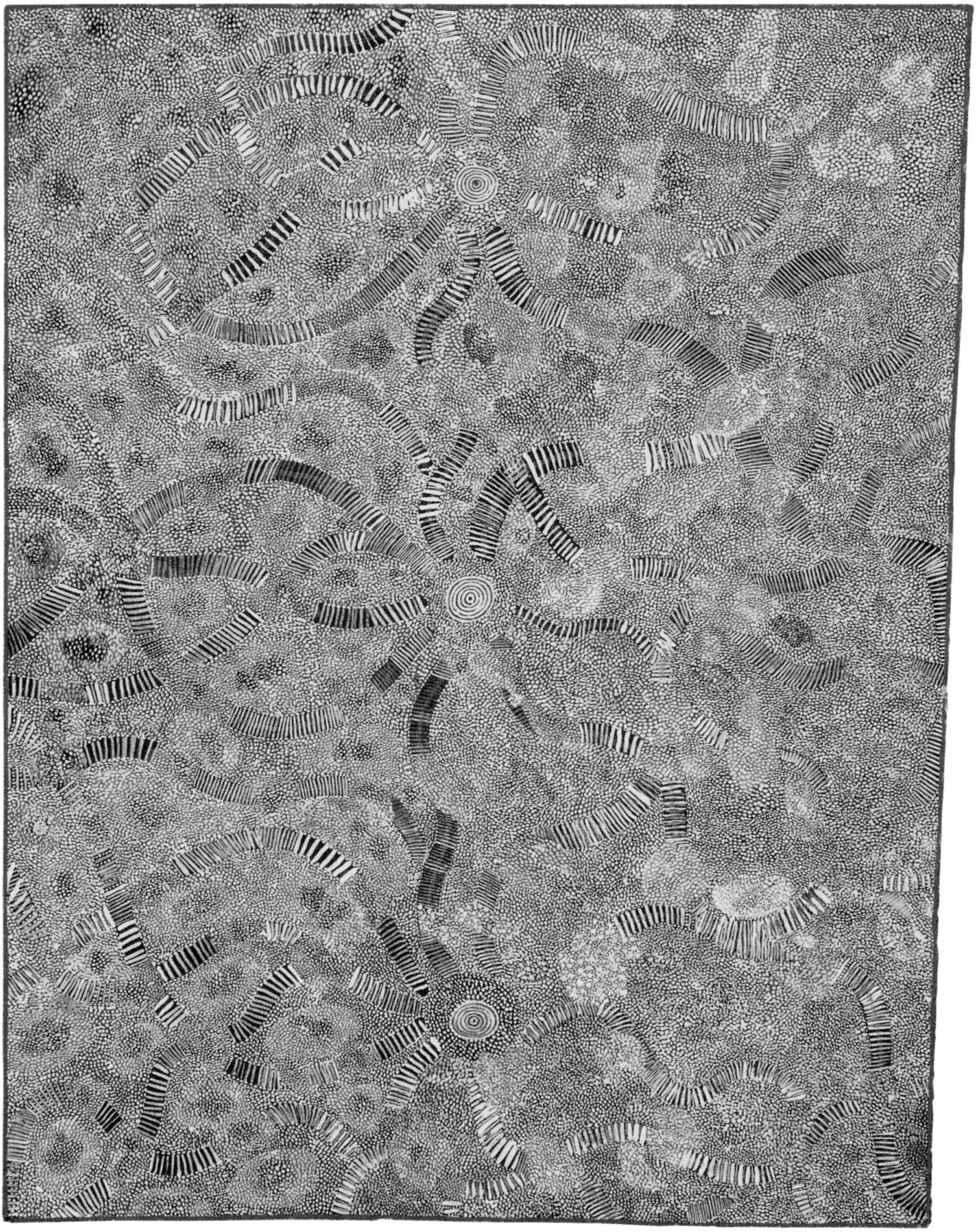

6.1 Kaapa Mbitjana Tjampitjinpa (with Tim Leura Tjapaltjarri), *Ngalyipi (A Small Snake)*, December 1972. Synthetic polymer powder paint on composition board, 121.92 × 95.25 cm.

DOTTING AND WEAVING

Kaapa Mbitjana Tjampitjinpa (with Tim Leura Tjapaltjarri),
***Ngalyipi (A Small Snake)*, 1972**

TS We should discuss at least one work by Kaapa Tjampitjinpa, given his importance during these early years. Two early paintings by Kaapa are in the Wilkerson collection: *Mikanji*, painted in October 1971, and *Budgerigar Dreaming (Version 1)*, 1972. Neither are included in this exhibition. They were shown in *Icons of the Desert*, but, on your advice, the curators consulted Kaapa's living relatives, who expressed concerns about the depictions of ceremonial figures and implements, so reproductions of them are included inside a supplement, inserted inside the back cover. In the Australian edition, the supplement is not included. The US edition alerts Aboriginal and Torres Strait Islander people who may chance upon the supplement that it includes "secret/sacred imagery which may be harmful to uninitiated members."[1]

No such imagery is evident in this painting. It is dated to December 1972. It clearly uses white dots to the full. It was made just a few months after Warangkula's great painting, so it may manifest his impact, even though a plethora of round dots is used rather than his delicate stippling effects. It is also measurably bigger than our other five paintings. As we look at it here in the

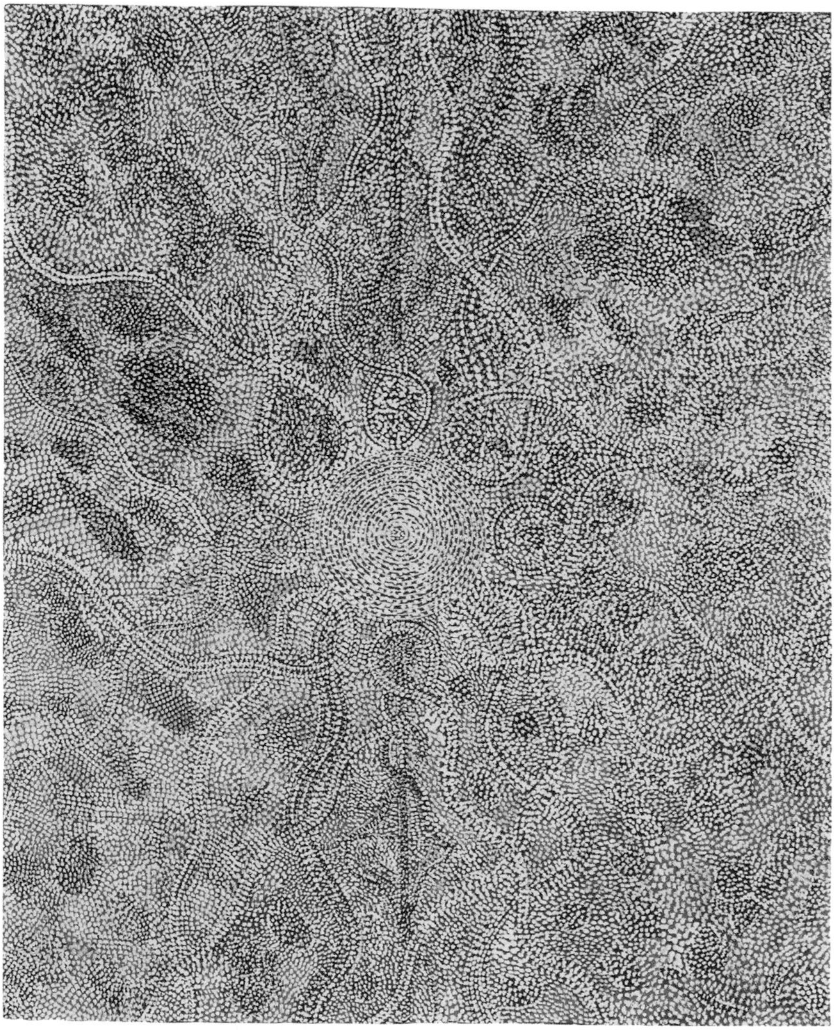

6.2 Tim Leura Tjapaltjarri, *Bushfire Spirit Dreaming at Napperby* (formerly *Untitled*), late 1972. Synthetic polymer paint on composition board, 60.64 × 47.94 cm. © Estate of the artist | Aboriginal Artists Agency Ltd.

residence, it is exhibited so that the light from the East River really brings out the dazzle.

FM Kaapa? Something about it suggests Tim Leura Tjapaltjarri to me. It is very like Tim Leura's *Bushfire Spirit Dreaming at Napperby* (formerly *Untitled*), also painted in late 1972 and in the Wilkerson collection.[2]

Does the *Icons* book say anything about Tim Leura?

TS [*reads*] "Probably assisted by Tim Leura Tjapaltjarri."[3] Right on, Fred.

They cite Peter Fannin's notes from the time naming it "Ngalyilpi (small snake) story." Next line says: "Place in the Spinifex (*tjanpi*) country well north of Yuendumu."[4] He also notes that Kaapa was "unwontedly reluctant to talk about this painting" and that Billy Stockman said that it was "dangerous" to do so.

FM Oh. . . . There's something about that translation and spelling of "Ngalyilpi" that's not making sense to me. The spelling needs to be changed from "Ngalyilpi" to "Ngalyipi" to get the title right. In Pintupi, the word *ngalyipi* usually names a fiber.[5] It's a plant that women twist into string. They use these to carry objects, like a rope, and to carry *coolamons* [carved wooden trays] in a shoulder sling. It is sometimes called "snake vine" [*Tinospora smilacina*], so perhaps that's where Fannin's understanding came from, but the reluctance to speak about it tells us that there are deeper levels, restricted understandings, masked perhaps by the relationship of *ngalyipi* and snakes. But there's also possibly a major ceremonial significance, relating to initiatory ceremonial activity, that we are not authorized to discuss. When Dick Kimber inquired about this painting, in consulting for the *Icons* exhibition, he says he "instantly discovered that my perception of a vine was incorrect for the particular painting even though there was a ropelike nature to the story." Kaapa's son explained, "*Ngalyipi*. That one dangerous again. Like 'business way' [referring to men's initiation]. Only man."[6] But I know that there are numerous versions of this painting done by each of these three men (Kaapa, Tim, Clifford).

TS Okay, so we can't delve too far into the story. Let's say what we can see by just looking. Most obviously, there is a multiplicity of long, thin forms coming from outside the painting's limits, twisting over, under, and through each other.

This is certainly a swarming, but I don't see any overtly snakelike figures, except perhaps the heads of the shapes that may be trying to enter the central circles. Presumably, these would be the snake's dens, on this reading.

FM The white banding on some of the wavy shapes makes them look segmented.

TS I see. In that sense, they invoke the idea of the skin of snakes. Lots of "small snakes" in a pit, perhaps. But this sense is contradicted by the size of the work, the power of some of these shapes, especially the ones that converge on the three sets of circles, which form a line down the middle, and set up the overall dynamic of symmetry with many variations inside it. A structure we see emerging in these paintings over and over.

FM Unlike you, I read the tendrils as emanating *from* the three circular forms that stake out the central axis of this painting. This three-circle structure is typical of how both Kaapa and Tim Leura compose painting after painting. The circles are obviously places of importance, places of ceremony.

TS I wonder whether the division of labor was like this: Kaapa lays down the *kuruwarri*, the main lines of the Dreaming story, while Tim Leura does the dotting, then they both rework it. (A bit like what we are doing.)

FM Kean points out that Tim Leura liked very fluid colors and pale hues, which he got from Johnny Warangkula.[7] These two artists habitually use a very watered-down acrylic. They like the shading, the light touch. Tim Leura's work becomes more and more like that. So, I think that this painting has more of him in it than Kaapa, but the story might be one that Kaapa had more claim over. If it was Kaapa alone, he was, at this stage, bolder, more direct, more likely to try to show the story and its ceremonial objects without these subtle kinds of veiling. A painting such as *The Winparrku Serpents*, even though it was done later, in 1974, shows us what this one might have looked like before Tim Leura got to it.[8]

TS The comparison is striking. It reminds us of how generous these artists were in sharing their stories and aspects of their personal styles. At the same time, you can sense that watching the efforts of other artists spurred them on to do things they would not have done on their own.

FM On that score, I think we can see the impact here of another artist, Clifford Possum Tjapaltjarri. At the time, he was visiting Papunya more often and turning up to paint with the other men. He was already known for his carvings of snakes, some wrapped around tree branches. He painted several Snake Dreamings, including a remarkable one on a shieldlike shape. It is listed as *Untitled (Snake Dreaming)* and dated to 1972.[9] It is so different from

6.3 Kaapa Mbitjana Tjampitjinpa, *The Winparrku Serpents*, 1974. Synthetic polymer paint on canvas on board, 124 × 78 cm. State Art Collection, Gallery of Western Australia, Perth. © Estate of the artist | Aboriginal Artists Agency Ltd.

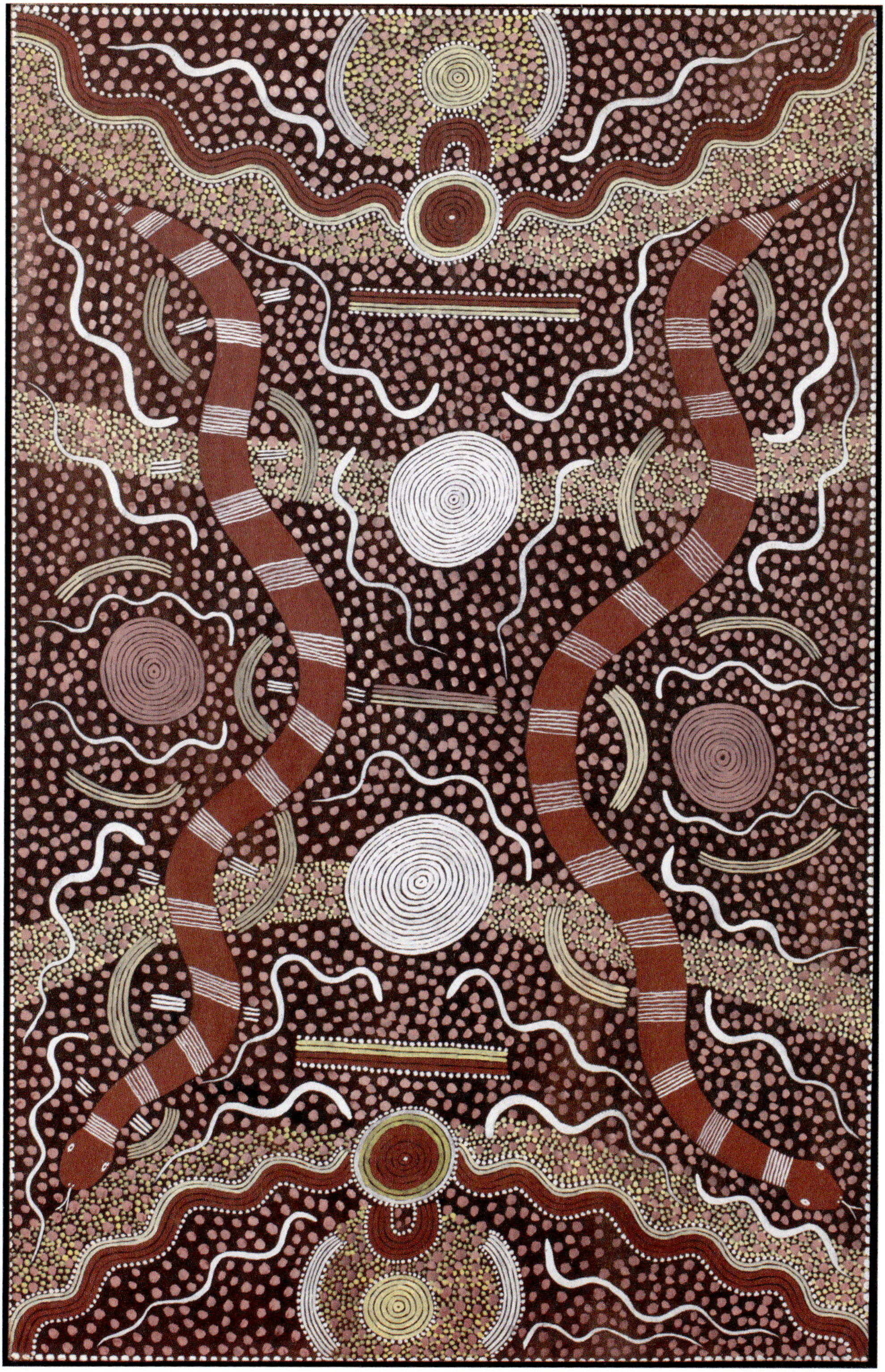

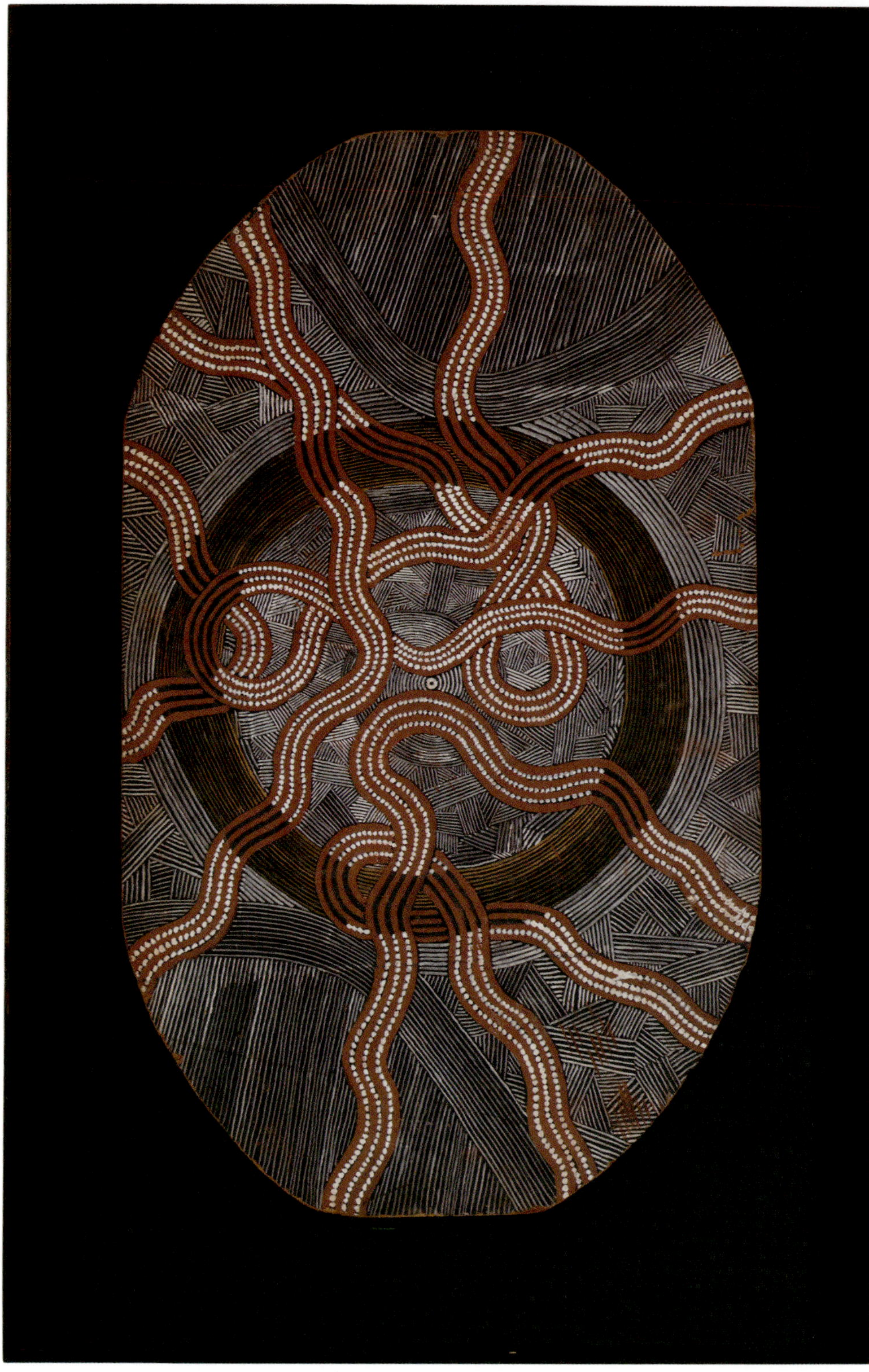

the painting we are looking at, yet they have a lot in common as well. It suggests there may be a template of some sort to represent the *Ngalyipi* story, since shields were commonly a platform on which designs were painted for various ceremonies.

TS Wow! Yes, allowing for the fact that we are looking at an image of it on an iPad, so we can't really sense the touch, truly feel the surface . . . the obvious difference is the use of dots. Except for a couple of spots inside the central circle, the entire ground has no dots. It is mostly patches of white stripes hatched over a black ground. They remind me of the kind of parallel lines often carved into the surfaces of shields, which usually evoke ancestral designs. But they could also simply evoke the sweeping movement of wind or snakes across sand. There are long streaks at the top and bottom as we look at it, and two sweeping curves around these areas. Perhaps the curves are shadowy allusions to men sitting for ceremony or are simply features of a place. Parallel lines also form a band around the huge black circle. Without knowing what each shape evokes, it is as if we were seeing the *Tjukurrpa* lines for *Ngalyipi*, the underlying structure of its central area, before the dotting was added.

The dots are almost totally confined to highlighting the slivering movement of the snakelike shapes: extrapolating from other paintings, these would be the tracks of the snakes moving through sand. Unlike the larger *Ngalyipi* painting, there is only one ceremonial place, presumably the area banded by the mainly black circle. The snake tracks wind their way into and out of this space. They don't seem to originate from it. The tiny white dot in what reads like the absolute center is actually the core of a large set of concentric circles. And they, in turn, are encircled by the black band and its surround. Fascinating that he studiously avoids dotting the sections where the snake tracks pass through—or is it under?—the black band. I suppose he is indicating a transition from one state to another, into a sacred place.[10]

FM It is a classic instance of the doubling I mentioned earlier, which we have seen at work in all the paintings we have discussed.

TS Right. In your essay for Stephen's exhibition *Everywhen* you define this doubling quite exactly. I am looking at a copy of the catalog. You say, "By dou-

6.4 Clifford Possum Tjapaltjarri, *Untitled (Snake Dreaming)*, 1972. Synthetic polymer powder paint on composition board, 78 x 45.5 cm. The Raschle Collection, Switzerland. © Estate of the artist | Aboriginal Artists Agency Ltd.

bling, I refer to the way in which an image can simultaneously be seen in two ways, as combining two perspectives, or be both past and present at once and not just shifting between two points of view."[11] The perspectives are those of the Dreaming and the noumenal world: their temporalities are contemporaneous. You focus on the *Children's Water Dreaming*, by Shorty Lungkarta, that we talked about earlier, version 2. (See fig. 2.2.) You comment that the doubling "does not subtract one exposure from another but combines them, overlays them, finds some way to put the different exposures together—a kind of everywhen."[12] So, this is not the basic duck-rabbit switcheroo, where a single image reads as one thing *or* another thing depending on what you take it to be. You can't see both at once.

FM No, it is something else, very hard to articulate. I end that essay wondering if the doubling might not also be understood as "a unity of disparate appearances and forms *as well as* the capacity to move between them."[13] How do we express *that*?

TS Let's home in on the capacity to move within this unity, within the doubling. To me, the key question is: What kinds of movement occur during this doubling? How do we experience it as we are looking? When ceremony is performed, the unity of the two worlds is right there, happening at once: marked-up bodies move in actual space, the ground paintings are sung, symbols and actions flash. But for these artists, setting out to evoke the presence of both places and the ceremonies that created them and re-create them, this is the key question: How do you trigger such doubled dimensions for viewers when your only resources are a flat surface, of limited physical dimensions, on which you can use a few specific symbols and a small repertoire of brushstrokes, by applying a medium that dries up soon after you apply it? All the crazy constraints without which the *kardiya* cannot see the value of what you put in front of them.

In our conversation, we have been trying to grasp the ways each of these painters confronted this challenge, so distinctively, while learning much from each other, before the broad patterns of Papunya style were set during the 1980s. One thing we have been doing throughout is track implied movements of various kinds within each painting. Perhaps this is the clue . . .

FM Maybe . . . but what kind of movement? Is this where words hit the wall when it comes to visual art?

TS A great place to be. I want to go back to our earlier discussion of the possible interactions between the painters in that room during that wet winter . . . especially to what might be occurring as Johnny Warangkula and Clifford Possum watched each other at work. We spoke of the energies evoked within *Water Dreaming at Kalipinypa*, the simultaneity of ancestral action converging on that place and the natural forces that sweep through it. Of course, the ancestral presence is recurrent, the natural forces are seasonal, thus also recurrent. We saw that Warangkula worked out a way of conveying both, by setting out a complex array of symbolic forms, then animating them through his extraordinarily subtle array of painted stipples. Meanwhile, Clifford Possum turns up. We can see in a couple of the Jensen photographs the third painting he did in the room, the *Honey Ant Ceremony*.[14]

I recall seeing this painting in Adelaide, at the Art Gallery of South Australia. It was hung as the centerpiece of a wall full of paintings from Papunya and Hermannsburg, underscoring the precedence of the painters at the mission and the movement of these artists between both places. Lisa Slade, the curator, told me that she often exhibited the two pencil and watercolor drawings that Namatjira made of his Yalka [yam] Dreaming totem in 1948 on either side of this painting. Which makes so much sense: the schematic format that Namatjira used in the 1940s is reinvented, or revived, by the next generation, by Clifford Possum and Tim Leura especially.[15] But whereas Namatjira was describing the totems, and their disposition on ceremonial boards, such that he might evoke the stories through voice, speaking or singing them, so they might be heard, or taken down as a record, Clifford Possum and Tim Leura aimed to evoke the stories by setting their signs in motion—within, we might say, the silence of the painted board.

The painters whose work we have been discussing each arrived at a different template for going beyond the formula developed by Kaapa in 1971. They each worked out a distinctive way of precipitating movement between the two states of being. In Adelaide, this hit me when I compared Clifford Possum's *Honey Ant Ceremony* with a Kaapa, painted the year before, which was hanging nearby.[16] It was one of those sent to Alice Springs for the Caltex Prize that year. Several ceremonial figures, objects, and tracks, signs, and depictions, each carefully delineated, were laid out on a black ground, in diagrammatic, even heraldic fashion. The doubling here is relatively straightforward: this is the look of the ceremony as created by the ancestors *and* as subsequently performed by their descendants. We know that by 1972 such explicit depictions were strongly discouraged, not only by Bardon, but also

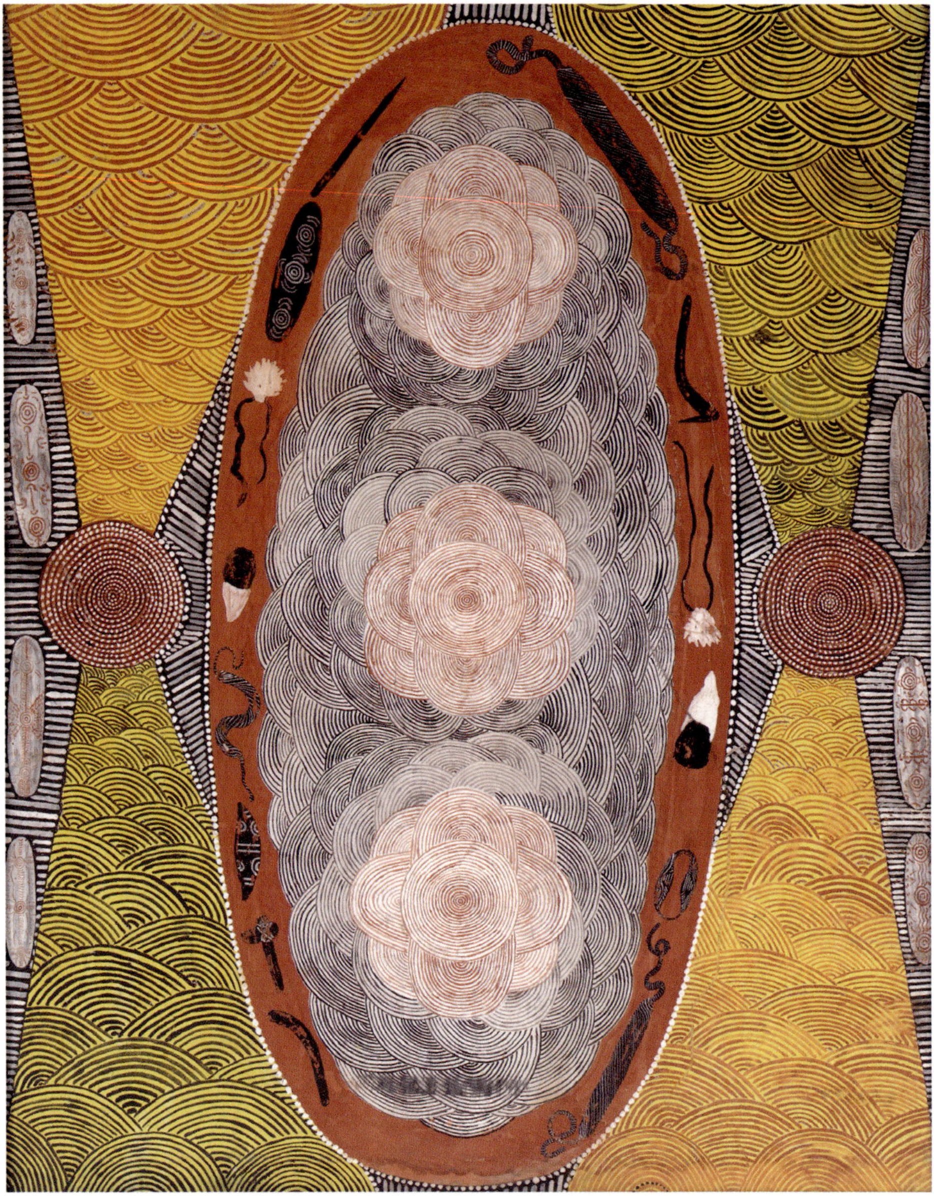

6.5 Clifford Possum Tjapaltjarri, *Honey Ant Ceremony*, 1972. Synthetic polymer paint on board, 104 × 81.4 cm. Elder Wing Centenary Gift of the Foundation 2001. Art Gallery of South Australia, Adelaide. © Estate of Clifford Possum Tjapaltjarri / Aboriginal Artists Agency.

by people at Yuendumu and elsewhere. A politics of the secret obligated these artists to find artistic languages for a poetics of the secret.

Clifford Possum had already produced some consummate "School of Kaapa" paintings: his *Emu Corroboree Man* and his *Rain Dreaming Dance*, both with prominent figures in ceremonial markings, done earlier in the year, before he had absorbed the restrictions. I see him as taking an important step in this painting, *Honey Ant Ceremony*. The execution is as precise as Kaapa's. Every line is as carefully drawn, perhaps more so. Everywhere, a similar, even consistency of application. Every thing, each part, is clearly distinguished. But the overall effect is nowhere near as static. The ceremonial objects within the trim of the red oval are drawn in the same descriptive way, it is true. But everything else has doubled, overlaid, shifting meanings. Everything is at once still yet in implied motion.

If we look at the painting, starting from the outside in, the eight ovoid shapes, presumably representing sacred, ceremonial objects, four on each side, might also be gestural sketches for ground paintings. The two sets of concentric circles at either side are, doubtless, a place of significance in the Dreaming track that runs through many of the major sites of the region. Typically, it is one place, repeated, respecting Anmatyerr symmetry of the supernatural and the natural.[17] The wedges of whorls radiating out from this place also seem to run toward it, up and down both sides, emanations of sacred energy spreading out but also contracting into the site. The red band is shieldlike in shape while also defining an area within a sand painting, within the ceremonial ground. The implements spin around within its border. But the main energy of the painting undoubtably comes from the three shapes that make up the central axis, that core we see in so many of his paintings, and in Tim Leura's, as you point out. Yet they are unusual. . . .

FM Yes, I am looking up Bardon's notations to see what he says. . . . He calls it *Honey Ant Dreaming (Version 3)*, same date, 1972, location, Napperby Station. He says, "The use of the oval form containing overlapping whorls in patterned rosette decoration seems to disguise any openness of motif."[18] It seems that Clifford Possum did not tell him much, or warned him off recording it. The artist did, however, speak a lot to Vivien Johnson when she was preparing her book on him. She says that the shapes depict "the underground nests of the Honey Ants as evacuated by an ancestral woman," and that her pubic belt and digging stick appear among the implements in the red border.[19]

TS "As evacuated": that's very interesting, a lot more than calling them "rosettes" and "decoration." When you look at the actual painting close-up, the plain handling could lead you to see those astonishing shapes as sitting on the surface, on the same plane as everything else. But step back just a little and each of the three central roundels becomes the apex of an agitated pile of red, overlapping whorls, themselves arising from a clustering of black whorls that sit on yet another layer of whorls, seemingly infinite in depth. The ancestral woman has certainly dug deep under the roots of a mulga bush to release the ants! She is not shown: only the effects of her actions, which are explosive.

No ants are depicted in what Bardon calls their "European" form, reflecting his strictures against this "whitefella" mode. But their luscious abundance as they hang in their chambers is vividly evoked, so strongly that the painting, especially the central section, seems to pulsate.

FM It is unusually intense and compacted, yes. To me, the whiteness here again suggests the effect of eagle-down fluff or vegetable-down fluff that is affixed to bodies for ceremony (*anteth* in Anmatyerr; *wamulu* in Pintupi) and flies everywhere during the performance. When it is used in ground paintings, it moves in the wind. John Kean has some powerful passages on Tim Leura's efforts to suggest this experience in his paintings of this period.[20]

TS Right on. In this painting we sense the energy of the woman digging, and the succulence of the ants, while at the same time being reminded of the dazzle of the ceremony being performed with great energy by the ancestors and their descendants—without any of these stories or events being directly depicted in a mimetic way.

From a technical point of view, it is remarkable that all this movement is conveyed through simple markings, economically applied, one layer on a given ground, with no devices to create the illusion of depth. True, the overlapping of the whorls triggers our eye's urge to complete them by sliding them out from the overlap, thus suggesting depth. But it is shallow and local. The main movement in and out of depth mostly results from the ambiguity within each whorl as to whether the white has been applied over the red and the black or vice versa. Close looking tells us that it is white on top in every case within the oval, with the brighter color on top in each of the lateral sections.

Pardon the pedantry, but such fine-tuning with color and line is as much an element in the Papunya aesthetic—indeed, in Indigenous art across the continent—as anything else we have discussed. It is a key to Clifford Possum's brilliance, as a painter and as a painter of brilliance.

FM Clifford Possum's love of working with visual puzzles comes out especially in the many paintings of Snake Dreamings that he made. I have just found another online. *Two Snakes at Alinitti*, 1972. It's a very elaborated version of the story about the snakes entering and leaving a waterhole.[21]

TS Wow again! The swipes are used to great effect in this one, the whites are highlighted, and whole sections of them are in bright yellow.[22] But the most striking thing is just how heraldic the overall composition is, yet how dynamically detailed it is within its pretty stiff symmetries and rigid repetitions. I mean, this template could repeat itself forever, in every direction. It takes up Kaapa's orderly way of setting out the ceremonial objects and places on neutral, one-color grounds but stretches it to infinity.[23] And Johnny Warangkula's way of gathering the several elements of a place into an intense accumulation is also there. The dynamic is so diagrammatic. You are absorbed in the detail but, at the same time, pushed away, out, and up. You can sense the big-scale, many-storied paintings to come.

FM Yes, the same is true of *Ngalyipi*, the painting in front of us. It also shares another key aspect that enabled what John Kean identified as the next great leap forward among these artists: the white dotting that seems, in some places, to push the forms beneath what we can see. John writes especially about the stippling and its affordance from the new polymer paints and the capacity to recall or resonate with ceremonial decorative effects. But I am reminded of other paintings by Clifford Possum where you're positioned as looking down from above, seeing the land below as if through clouds.

TS Yes, one example of that is in the collection: *Women's Dreaming about Bush Tucker, Yarlga*, dated to this time, late 1972.[24] The signs from the stories are laid down first, as is usual, but the sections that are background or infill in other paintings now float freely, like clouds in Japanese screen paintings. The irregular white overlays in that painting might be smoke from a bushfire. But some clusters of dots are clearly patches of ground or of vegetation. He sets these into floating motions as well. This is abstraction. The result is that we see fragments of the Dreaming narratives beneath. . . .

Ha! "Content is a glimpse." That's a famous saying of Willem de Kooning, the great American Abstract Expressionist painter. A very different kind of

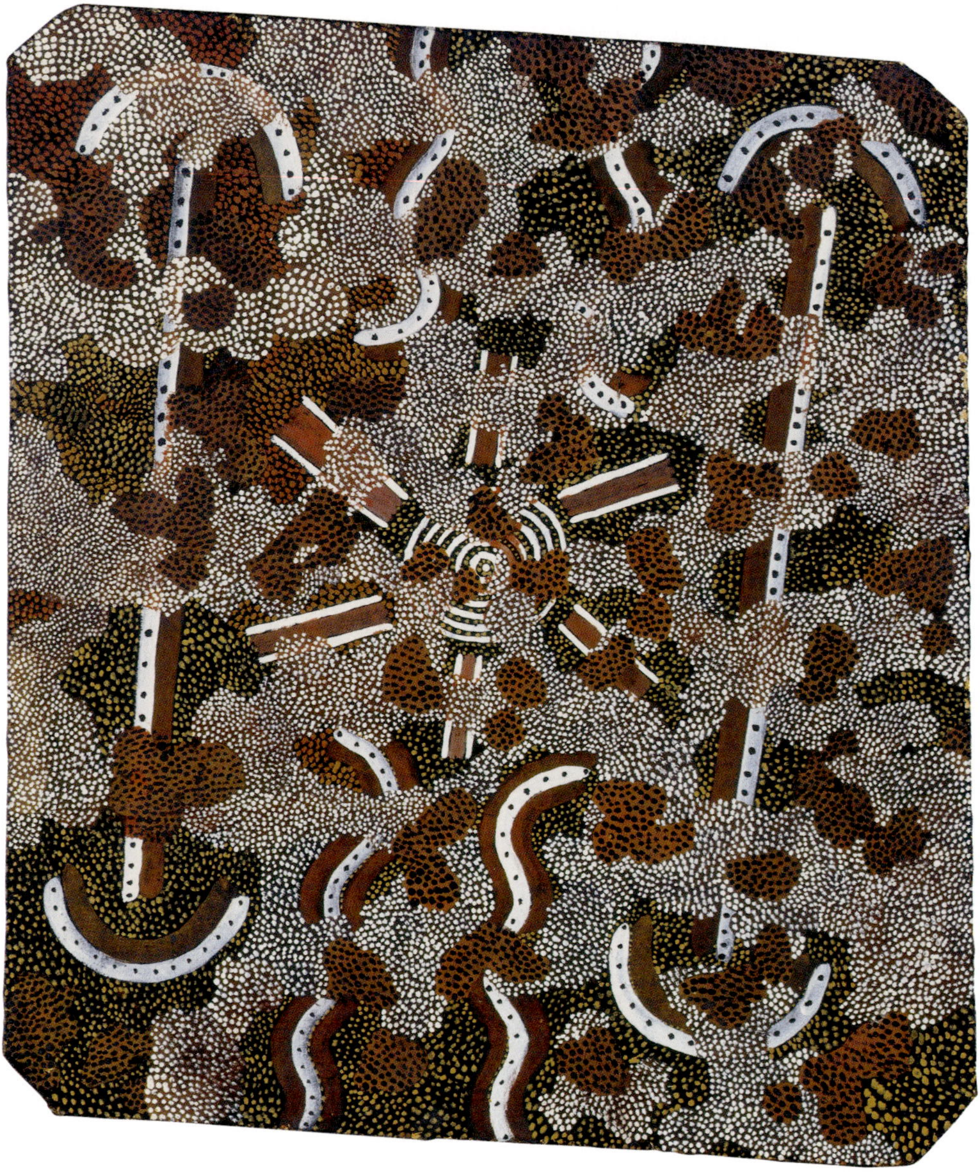

6.6 Clifford Possum Tjapaltjarri, *Women's Dreaming about Bush Tucker, Yarlga*, 1972. Synthetic polymer/powder paint on composition board, 64.45 × 55.56 cm. © Estate of the artist | Aboriginal Artists Agency Ltd.

content, in this case. This is one of Clifford Possum's several ways of working through the conceal/reveal pictorial logic that so many of these artists wrestled with so inventively at this time. It certainly has been one of the major themes of our conversation.

He and his brother Tim Leura went on to make many paintings that took up these ideas and expanded on them, to great effect. They invoked movement through vast stretches of country, crisscrossed by several storylines. No accident that they were now painting on canvas, which is in principle limited only by stretcher support and wall space. There are famous ones such as *Warlugulong*, a Fire Dreaming interlaced with other stories, from 1976. I still recall its impact at the *Australian Perspecta* exhibition at the Art Gallery of New South Wales in Sydney in 1981. *Perspecta* was national in scope, the biennial survey of contemporary Australian art. *Warlugulong* was shown in the same space as Tim Leura's *Spirit Dreaming through Napperby Country* painting of 1980—which, by the way, is anchored along its great length by six clusters of circles, painted, I believe, by Clifford—and Charlie Tjapangati's *Tingari Dreaming*, 1981, one of the major early "map" paintings that became so prominent in the 1980s. Bernice Murphy, the curator, interspersed these three with two paintings by David Aspden, a leading abstract painter based in Sydney. He had mastered the creation of fields of color through the juxtaposition of ragged patches of pure color.[25] We were surprised to see that one of them, *Big Red*, 1980, used natural ochre colors, staples in Aboriginal art, as we called it then. And in his other painting, *Raising the Sky*, 1981, he used similar colors but also took on the "overview" space that these artists were deploying in their multiple story paintings. If my memory serves me correctly, Bernice hung *Big Red* next to *Warlugulong*, and *Raising the Sky* close to *Spirit Dreaming through Napperby Country*. They were of similar dimensions; the first two were big squares, the other two long rectangles.

She was doing more than drawing attention to formal resonances between paintings. She was positing their equivalence as *artists of consequence*. And more: a major non-Indigenous artist was seeking to learn from fellow artists, whom he had the wit to see as masters of his kind of art.

This was the first time that Indigenous artists had been included in a survey of contemporary Australian art.[26] Somehow, it was instantly convincing. It converted those who still regarded Aboriginal art as a lesser, imitative phenomenon or, at best, as an aberration, a kind of art historical fluke. An unforgettable moment . . .

FM There have been many such moments since then.

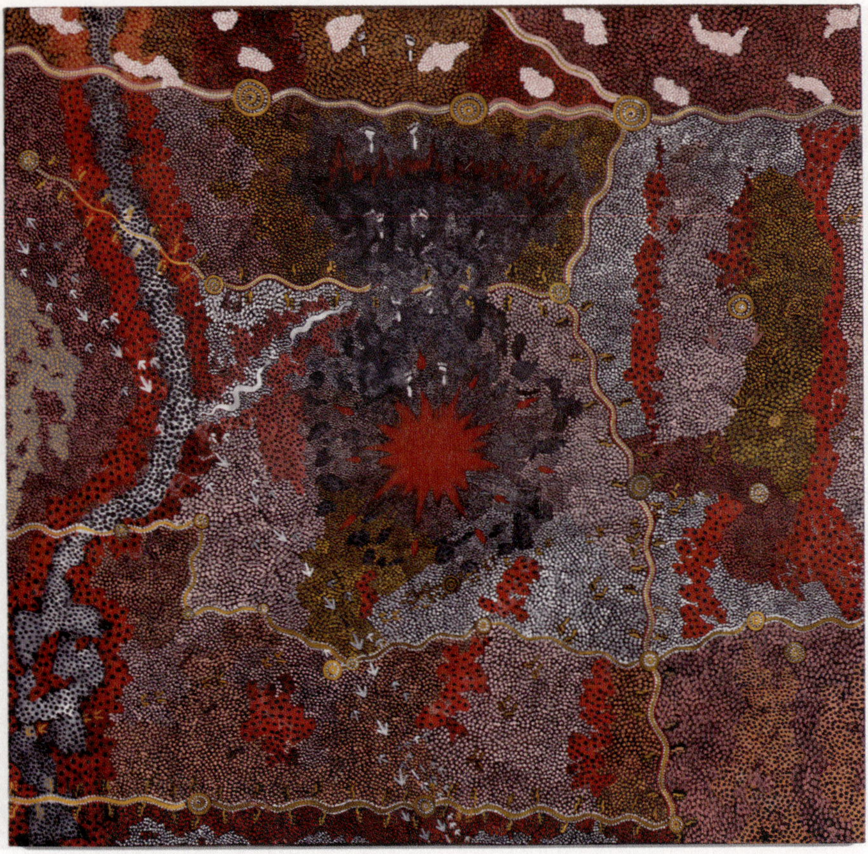

6.7 Clifford Possum Tjapaltjarri, *Warlugulong*, 1976. Synthetic polymer paint on canvas, 168.5 × 170.5 cm. Art Gallery of New South Wales, Sydney. © Estate of the artist | Aboriginal Artists Agency Ltd.

TS Yes, indeed. Getting back to this painting before us, I am still puzzled over some of the internal detail. At some places there are clusters of tiny white dots, like spores—the three in the top right corner, for example, or those in the lower right quadrant. Art advisor Peter Fannin's diagram says that they are clumps of spinifex.[27]

I also wonder about the title *A Small Snake*. Obviously, if the wavy lines are snakes, there are many of them. They don't seem so small.[28] The lines also flow into and, as you say, out of the circles as well as in and out of the implied ground, as if they were being woven into it. Perhaps, then, the painting is a visualization of the fiber itself being woven in ceremony or, better put, of the work that *Ngalyipi* does when it weaves this world and the Dreaming together during an initiation.

FM I may be way overboard on this, but I know that some anthropologists have pointed out, for Warlpiri culture, hair string, made from human hair, as used in ceremonies, can symbolize or represent the uterus, women's reproductive power. The association of *ngalyipi* with women (as women's equivalent to hair string) suggests such a deep connection. I never found anyone who would discuss this with me, for obvious reasons.

TS Weaving is the basic pictorial logic of this painting, as in many of the others, and of so many to come, although in different ways. Each of the stories they tell unfold through time: the ancestral beings went in and out of the ground; they enter in one place, appear in another. Ceremonies reenact this world-making process. It has been going on for millennia.

The small selection of paintings we have discussed shows us how these artists laid the groundwork for the extraordinary outburst that followed.

We have reached the limits of what we can know through our ways of looking at what these six paintings have offered. And from the knowledge shared verbally by the artists and gleaned by others. A good place for us to stop speaking.

SIX PAINTINGS FROM PAPUNYA: A REFLECTION

Stephen Gilchrist

REVELATION AND CONCEALMENT are significant philosophical couplets for Indigenous art and culture. In the thoughtful conversation recorded between art historian Terry Smith and anthropologist Fred Myers, they look at a number of paintings from the John and Barbara Wilkerson collection that typify the inventive power of art from Papunya, a government settlement located 240 kilometers (150 miles) northwest of Alice Springs, in the symbolic heart of Australia. In 1971–72, a group of male artists began creating small paintings on boards that chronicled epic ancestral narratives that were encoded within customary law. These works presented a powerful visual language that had never been seen by outside audiences and revolutionized the way in which non-Indigenous people related to the Western Desert, the continent of Australia, and the towering systems of knowledge that it contains. Their extraordinary paintings that represented "Country"—a colloquialism of Aboriginal English meaning culturally inherited tracts of land—were striking in their creative and ancestral vitality. As art historian Roger Benjamin says,

> Beauty has many forms, but it is not every day that a new kind of beauty is born to the world. Such is the achievement of the painters from Papunya. Theirs was a strange beauty, unlike anything seen before by the white

> people who were among its first admirers. On small rectangles of cheap brown Masonite, they wove intricate traceries of waving lines, circles, and dots. Their painting forms were not haphazard; instead, they had the inestimable advantage of drawing on millennia of culture and tradition.[1]

The legacy of these small boards is undeniable as they ultimately facilitated a growing receptiveness to the art practices of Indigenous people and the need for political and cultural self-determination. This movement, which began as the domain of mostly senior men, has been revitalized by their wives, sisters, and daughters—as well as their sons, grandsons, and nephews—who continue to convey sanctioned aspects of their cultural knowledge to global audiences.

Art has been one of the most crucial platforms for Indigenous people from Australia to make legible their own creative and cultural concerns. But the knowledge that it holds has often been assimilated into non-Indigenous frameworks, which can diminish its full intercultural capacity. The newness of this art to non-Indigenous people seemed to license new definitional regimes that ultimately brought such encounters with Indigenous art too prematurely to their conclusion. In many ways, Indigenous artists created the conditions for art historical and anthropological discourse, but they were not generally recognized as theoreticians. This Western conceit permitted the dismissal or devaluation of Indigenous systems of theorization. As Mohawk scholar Audra Simpson and academic Andrea Smith acknowledge in their justification for a theorization of Native studies, "Racialized and colonial Others become marked as those who can be theorized about, but not those who can theorize."[2] But due to the sheer force of these paintings and the personalities of their makers, this silencing could never be condoned. Alternatives were found by those who were willing to enter into the participatory and sensorial worlds of these paintings and of their creators. Fred and Terry are two such individuals. Their careers are testament to their ability to work with Indigenous artists and to take seriously the work of translating it for others.

As Fred and Terry viewed the Papunya works on display in New York, it was clear that the paintings actively created and signaled their own cultural coordinates that open up thresholds of Country, knowledge, and sacred power. Through their patient physical and intellectual engagement with these works of art, new and ancient knowledge was communicated to Fred and Terry. Exploring the interpretive possibilities of form and content, they move from fine dotting to cosmological significations in an effort to understand the paintings on their symbolic, familial, cultural, aesthetic, and political levels. The lengthy discussions are highly attentive to the technical innovations of the artists, their inventive and exploratory imagery, the rich cultural signification of the paintings, and, occasionally, their unutterable ceremonial associations.

Throughout their discussions, ideas are shared, tested, elaborated, revisited, and sometimes shut down out of deference to cultural politics. Applying and respecting the requisite cultural protocols is an important extension of Indigenous critical care and value. This is readily and unproblematically given by the authors. Methodological and critical tools from their respective disciplines of art history and anthropology are brought to bear on their discussions, but these are used to facilitate a form of generative wayfinding rather than imposing a predetermined outcome. Through their enthusiastic collaboration, they model a particular analytical mode that is still rare but is becoming increasingly necessary. Over the course of these discussions, disciplinary mutualities become more pronounced and the differences are rendered benign. Fred and Terry understand that Indigenous art and culture is utterly disinterested in upholding disciplinary monopolies of power. Instead, they embrace ideas of interconnectedness, holism, and reciprocity that are more resonant to Indigenous peoples. In many ways, these values are also aligned with contemporary approaches to multidisciplinarity that are also imparted through this exchange.

To appreciate the innovative nature of this discussion, it is perhaps necessary to briefly note the histories that both disciplines have played in both defining and confining Indigenous art. Bundjulung curator Djon Mundine dramatizes these disciplinary orientations as tournaments taken up between the imperial Houses of Anthropology and Art History.[3] Putting aside more complex genealogies and methodologies, an art historical approach could broadly be described as one that privileges the formal qualities of a work of art while an anthropological approach is one that situates the work within a localized cultural and social context. While these are often presented as oppositional methodologies, elsewhere Fred has reminded us that "[art] criticism has significant parallels with anthropology as an interpretive activity which has culture as its object."[4] Similarly, Nicholas Thomas suggests the possibility of doing "anthropological art history."[5] Appreciation of these similarities between the disciplines is much rarer than identifying the differences.

The literature is crowded with denunciations of anthropology by Indigenous artists and curators, and often in its place there is an eager alignment to the values of fine art or contemporary art. This meaningful, intentional, and ongoing shift toward new intermediary categories must be seen as a defection from the discipline of anthropology, its much larger body of literature, and its legacy of temporal deceits. Although the period of art historical engagement with Indigenous art is much shorter, it has proven to be no less insensitive, and Indigenous art must be eternally vigilant toward its co-option into art history. Inclusion, it must be said, is not equity.

The self-serving debates about the merit of particular approaches eventually exhausted themselves. What became apparent to some, but what was always there, is that Indigenous art is already self-possessed of its own value. It is necessary to apprehend it on its own cultural terms. This obvious but radical reorientation should generate more nuanced scholarship that is attuned to Indigenous cultural values.

Shifting frameworks takes courage, and it also takes time. The discussions that the reader of this conversation is privy to show a possible way forward. What these real-time encounters reveal is that Fred and Terry have expended considerable intellectual and physical time with these works of art. Furthermore, they have spent time building relationships with the artists in order to be able to ask the right questions and to receive the knowledge available to them. It is, of course, important to note that Indigenous systems of knowledge are based not on what can be known but on who can know certain things and at what juncture. Unlike Western forms of universal knowledge, Indigenous information cannot be shared equally, not even within a wholly Indigenous context. Fred and Terry shoulder the ethical responsibilities that issue from these relationships and respect the differential registers of knowledge. Inscribing Indigenous protocols into dominant fields of art is not just an intervention into conventional modes of practice but a vivification of Indigenous cultural modalities.

Indigenous art has historically put pressure on and forced an expansion of the definitional regimes in which it is positioned and of the institutional spaces that it takes up. For me, this demonstrates the smallness of the conceptual, racial, and aesthetic categories in which Indigenous art and artists have been and are now permitted to occupy. Throughout this conversation, however, there is a commitment to troubling the limits of critical language and exceeding the categories of Indigenous art as they have been understood and positioned. Dispensing with these limitations, the authors fall deeper and deeper into the geographical, cultural, political, and cosmological dimensions of these works. What is striking about the conversation between Fred and Terry is that they recognize the vastness and at times the incommensurability of Indigenous art.

This responsiveness to the depth of Indigenous art and culture and the willingness to shift frameworks can be seen in the expansionary nature of some of the chapter titles themselves, which reference important philosophical ideas of spirituality, eternality, temporality, the politics of knowledge, and abundance. While Fred and Terry appreciate that Indigenous art is in tacit dialogue with dominant approaches to categorization, their conversations work to reduce this determinative power. There is no desire to coax these paintings into familiar and complacent categorizations. On the contrary, they are genuinely responding to the intellectual and cultural challenges of the paintings by shaping a critical vocabulary and methodology that can best apprehend them. Visual and technical comparisons are made more often to other Indigenous artists than to Western artists. Presenting these new terms of reference is hugely consequential.

In his essay "Currents of World-Making in Contemporary Art," Terry presents the following contextualization of intercultural encounters, which has produced, at least in theory, a redistribution of power. He observes: "As European and US-centric perspectives decline in dominance, and awareness of the agency of others penetrates even the cultural citadels of what used to be known as the First World, it becomes more and more difficult to maintain the presumption that art is in essence universal, its objects timeless and the experiences that it offers transcendental—in other words, that it is fundamentally *unworldly*."[6] Responding to this provocation, Fred and Terry demonstrate a cultural universe that is self-affirming and complete on its own terms. The crisis of hierarchical and ever-evolving definitions that has long characterized the critical reception of Indigenous art is of little relevance here. This doesn't mean that Indigenous art and culture is and should always be separate from the rest of the world. Rather it is suggested that it has its own rules of engagement and its own systems of valuation that need to be respected and absorbed. These questions and many others have sustained the intellectual interests of Fred and Terry over many years. Being witness to their active mediation of objects that honors the artists, the memory of place, and the narratives that are embedded in them, they show us the richness of Indigenous cultural practices and the tools with which to apprehend them. Indigenous art and culture deserve nothing less.

Belonging to the Yamatji people of the Inggarda language group, **Dr. Stephen Gilchrist** is senior lecturer in the School of Indigenous Studies at the University of Western Australia. He is a writer and curator who has worked with the Indigenous Australian collections of the National Gallery of Australia, the British Museum, the National Gallery of Victoria, and the Hood Museum of Art at Dartmouth College. He has curated numerous exhibitions in Australia and the United States and has written extensively on Indigenous art from Australia. From 2012 to 2016 he was the Australian Studies Visiting Curator at the Harvard Art Museums, Harvard University, for which he curated the exhibition *Everywhen: The Eternal Present in Indigenous Art from Australia*. He works with major Australian and international institutions and contributes to the international dialogues surrounding the scholarship and interpretation of Indigenous art and culture with a focus on Indigenous curation as an expression of sovereignty.

Language and Person Names

Language Names

Anmatyerr
Arrernte
Luritja
Pintupi
Pitjantjatjara
Warlpiri, also Walpiri or Walbiri

Names of Persons

It was not unusual during the mid-twentieth century for Indigenous people in Australia to be known by several names or combinations of names. Wartuma (Charlie Tarawa/Tjaruru) Tjungurrayi, for example, was known by a number of different names, particularly to the non-Indigenous people, some perhaps from mishearing or misspelling but also because personal names are not used commonly in Indigenous communities and other appellations commonly replace them. Thus, Wartuma had come to be known as "Charlie," probably based on his reported early meeting of Charles Duguid at Hermannsburg, and as Charlie Tjaruru (with *Tjaruru* being a section name, and one that is related to his subsection Tjungurrayi) and then possibly a mishearing of *Tjaruru*, as Charlie Tarawa. These names were often used to record his presence in government documents, mission censuses, or other records. Wartuma, however, was the name by which he was most known in his own community. Similar processes underlie the various forms or spellings in which the names of painters have been recorded.

Glossary

Churinga/tjurunga/tjuringa/twyerrenge: Different spellings of the word used to describe certain kinds of men's sacred objects.

Claypan: Also known as *maluri*, a temporary water source in the desert where water gathers after rain and remains on the surface. Such an area is also sometimes called a "swamp." Such places provided opportunities for people to gather in seasons when vegetable food would be abundant from the water.

Honey ants (*tjala, tjarla, yirrampa, ngari*): A species of ants that live in chambers under the ground and store honey in their abdomens. They are regarded as a delicacy and are dug up especially by women to share with their families.

Kuwarla: Frost; also *nyinnga*. Can refer to "ice," "extreme cold." Has been spelled as *G'wala* in some titles.

Mingatjurru: The golden bandicoot.

Ngalyipi: Snake vine, a creeping plant, twisted into a fiber that women use to carry *coolamon* (wooden dishes on which they can transport infants).

Ngurra: The Pintupi and Luritja word referring to "country" (as in a place), a "camp" (where people are living or have lived), or, more extendedly, "home" (including the "home" or place where an animal might live).

Ninu: Rabbit-eared bandicoot, bilby.

Puturru: Refers to hair string, usually made from human hair that has been cut and then spun into a string that can have various uses.

Tingarri: Sometimes spelled as *Tingari*, it is the name for mythological groups of senior men leading younger novices through travels across the landscape, conducting ceremonies of initiation, instruction, and acting in the world, making waterholes and the landscape through their actions, and modeling customs that continue to be followed as they are "*Tjukurrtjanu*," that is, "from The Dreaming."[1] The *Tingarri* are generally identified as part of the Pintupi repertoire, but other groups have stories that are identified as equivalents in their cycles of initiation. Stories from this cycle of events in the Dreaming came to be seen as acceptable to show in paintings, with restrictions in the level and sacredness of knowledge provided. The songs of the *Tingarri* ancestral beings are regarded as acceptable for noninitiated persons to hear. The catalog *Irritja Kuwarri Tjungu / Past and Present Together* (edited by Fred Myers and Henry Skerritt) illustrates some of the connected lines of ancestral places in *Tingarri* travels that were painted by Papunya Tula artists.

Tjanpi: Spinifex grass.

Tjukurrpa/"Dreaming": "The Dreaming" is a term made famous by the anthropologist W. E. H. Stanner in his 1956 essay of the same title, published in his book *White Man Got No Dreaming: Essays 1938–1973*. The term is used in English by many Indigenous people in Central Australia to translate the concept of what Pintupi and other Western Desert language speakers call *Tjukurrpa*, and many non-Indigenous commentators have continued to use it. Stanner wrote poetically of the metaphysical vision of Indigenous people:

> The truth of it seems to be that man, society and nature, and past, present and future, are at one together within a unitary system of such a kind that its ontology cannot illumine minds too much under the influence of humanism, rationalism, and science. One cannot easily, in the mobility of modern life and thought, grasp the vast intuitions of stability and permanence, and of life and man, at the heart of Aboriginal ontology.[2]

Tjukurrpa refers to a domain of being in which powerful ancestral beings gave the world its shape and meaning. Aboriginal ceremonies both reenact the events of the Dreaming and come from it. As Stanner reported, Aborigines say that in performing or revealing (*yutininpa*) the ceremonies they "follow The Dreaming," sometimes called "the Law."[3] Pintupi men repeatedly told Fred Myers of various customs, designs, practices, that they were "*Tjukurrtjanu, mularrarringu*," that is, were "from The Dreaming, they became real."[4] Knowledge of these events and their signs may be restricted, and the ceremonies are revelatory: they present the story of what happened at a particular place and how it shaped the geography there. Thus, they make available knowledge of fundamentally important and invisible events and structures. (Indeed, *Tjukurrpa* is held to contrast in some ways with that which is *yuti*—visible, hearable, or sensorily present.) It is these matters that the Papunya Tula artists use as their subjects in the acrylic paintings. Description of a painting as, for example, "Rain Dreaming" would mean that the story depicted involves the activities of an ancestral being associated with or identified with water or rain in the Dreaming, and would be expressed as *Kapi* (water, rain) *Tjukurrpa*.

Winpa: Lightning, the Lightning Man.

Yarlga: Bush onion.

Yuti: Clearly visible, clearly heard, clearly understood.

Yutinu: Revealed, shown.

Notes

Introduction

Epigraph: Long Jack Phillipus to Luke Scholes, Papunya, September 2010, cited in Luke Scholes, "Long Jack Phillipus Tjakamarra," in Ryan and Batty, *Tjukurrtjanu*, 92.

1. On the Western art-culture system, see Nelson Graburn, "Introduction: The Arts of the Fourth World," in Graburn, *Ethnic and Tourist Arts*, 1–32; and James Clifford, "On Collecting Art and Culture," in Clifford, *The Predicament of Culture*, 215–51. On the location of Indigenous Australian art within this system, see Myers, *Painting Culture*.

2. Scholars of the creative output of other Indigenous peoples in Australia offer insights of equivalent value, and richly suggestive parallels. For example, anthropologist Howard Morphy, in books such as *Ancestral Connections: Art and an Aboriginal System of Knowledge* and *Becoming Art: Exploring Cross-Cultural Categories*, identifies a range of subtle devices that nuance the use of certain templates derived from ceremonial markings on the body, and from designs used in rock and sand painting, when Yolngu artists addressed the challenge of how to present Dreaming imagery on the rectangular support of a section of bark cut from a tree. Other works that might be mentioned specifically in relation to the Central Australian movement include Carty, *Balgo*; Carty and French, "Art of Central Australia"; Brooks and Jorgensen, *Wanarn Painters of Place and Time*; and, for the Kimberley, Sprague, *The Stranger Artist*.

3. Gilchrist, "Indigenous Curatorial Interpellations," 254.

4. Landmark exhibitions by Indigenous curators include the following: Djon Mundine: *The Aboriginal Memorial* (1988), *Tyerabarrbowaryaou* [I shall never become a white man] (with Fiona Foley, 1994), and *The Native Born* (1996); Hetti Perkins: *Blak art* (1993), *Fluent: Emily Kame Kngwarreye, Yvonne Koolmatrie, Judy Watson* (1997), and *Papunya: Genesis and Genius* (2000); Brenda L. Croft: *Culture Warriors* (2007) and *Still in My Mind: Gurindji Location, Experience and Visuality*

(2017); Margo Neale: *Emily Kame Kngwarreye* (2008) and *Songlines: Tracking the Seven Sisters* (2021); and Stephen Gilchrist: *Everywhen: The Eternal Present in Indigenous Art from Australia* (2016).

5. Perkins and Fink, *Papunya Tula*.

6. Perkins, "Stories I Can Tell," 82.

7. Myers and Skerritt, *Irritjtja Kuwarri Tjungu*, 82.

8. Myers, "Traffic in Culture," 239.

9. Bardon and Bardon, *Papunya*, 17. For a detailed account of these events emphasizing the agency of the several people involved, see Kean, "Digging for Honey Ants."

10. Geoffrey Bardon, "A Selected Catalogue," in Bardon and Bardon, *Papunya*, 92–501.

11. The development of secondary market interest in these works is traced in Johnson, *Once Upon a Time in Papunya*, chap. 5.

12. John and Barbara Wilkerson, "Collectors' Foreword," in Benjamin, *Icons of the Desert*, 7.

13. Benjamin, *Icons of the Desert*, 21. At the time of this exhibition, there were fifty-eight Papunya paintings in the Wilkerson collection. Subsequently, ten more were acquired.

14. See Myers, "Paintings, Publics and Protocols."

15. Rey, "Bardon's Legacy." See also *Mr. Patterns*, dir. Catriona McKenzie (Film Australia, 2004, 55 min.).

16. Carter, "Introduction."

17. At the same time, there was some recognition that focusing on the "story," or the religious significance of the works, impeded their recognition as "art" in the prevailing discourses of the time. Bardon's successor as art advisor, Peter Fannin, recognized the importance of this in marketing the work. He conceived a special category, "fine art-ethnology," to elevate the work from the category of "tourist art." The "stories" were seen as important sources of value, but the productivity of the artists meant that the documentation imposed a huge stress, especially when the backlog of undocumented paintings prevented them from moving to market. The reason Fannin asked Myers to help with documentation at Yayayi in 1973 was because he, like Bardon, could not keep up with the output of paintings.

18. Bardon and Bardon, *Papunya*, 50–65.

19. Bardon and Bardon, *Papunya*, 239.

20. Carter, "Introduction," xvii. It seems likely that Bardon was aware of the anthropologist Nancy Munn's early work and publications on Walbiri sign systems. See Munn, "Walbiri Graphic Signs"; and Munn, "Visual Categories."

21. Bardon and Bardon, *Papunya*, 27.

22. Bardon and Bardon, *Papunya*, 30.

23. See the many examples in Phillips and Vorano, *Mediating Modernisms*. The colonial structure also obtains for non-Indigenous cultural mediators who were

not modernists, those who disseminated and interpreted Indigenous traditional and neotraditional cultural products.

24. See, for example, Hogan, "Notes and Inventory."

25. For example, the Boomalli Aboriginal Artists' Cooperative in inner-city Sydney, active since 1987. See Fordham and Duhrkoop, *Boomalli Prints and Paper*.

26. See French, *Seeing the Centre*; and McGregor, *The Life and Times of Albert Namatjira*.

27. Johnson, *Once Upon a Time in Papunya*, 18, and chaps. 1 and 2. Johnson has done invaluable work on the artists' biographies in *Aboriginal Artists of the Western Desert* and *Lives of the Papunya Tula Artists*, and through her monographs, *The Art of Clifford Possum Tjapaltjarri* and *The Art of Michael Nelson Jagamara*. The role of Kaapa has some parallels to individual Native American artists, as profiled in A. Ryan, *The Trickster Shift*. Peter Sutton has discussed other Australian examples of such mediators in *The Politics of Suffering*.

28. This book is based on his dissertation of the same title, submitted to the University of Melbourne in 2020. As it happened, we were both examiners of Kean's outstanding dissertation. Regarding the several people who had important roles in the developments at Papunya, see Scholes, "Unmasking the Myth."

29. See Edmond, *Battarbee and Namatjira*.

30. Colin Jack-Hinton, director of the Museum and Art Gallery of the Northern Territory, made this point in his book *Aboriginal Art Past and Present*, 19–20. See also Burn and Stephen, "Namatjira's White Mask"; and Smith, "Albert Namatjira and Margaret Preston."

31. *Untitled (Yalka no. 1)* and *Untitled (Yalka no. 2)* are in the collection of the Art Gallery of South Australia. They are plates 13 and 14 in his dissertation. He discusses them on pages 57–60. See also Kean, *Dot, Circle, and Frame*, 46–47 and plate 16.

32. Kean, "Dot, Circle, and Frame," i.

33. Kean, "Papunya," 7.

34. See his essay in Scholes, *Tjungu<u>n</u>utja*.

35. McLean, *How Aborigines Invented the Idea of Contemporary Art*, introduction, and in particular his essay on pages 333–45.

36. McLean, *Rattling Spears*, chap. 5.

37. Sid Anderson, Long Jack Phillipus Tjakamarra, Michael Nelson Jagamara AM, Joseph Jurra Tjapaltjarri, Bobby West Tjupurrula, and Desmond Phillipus Tjurpurrula with Luke Scholes, "Tjungu<u>n</u>utja (from Having Come Together)," in Scholes, *Tjungu<u>n</u>utja*, 117–27.

38. Scholes, *Tjungu<u>n</u>utja*, 119.

39. Scholes, *Tjungu<u>n</u>utja*, 118.

40. Scholes, *Tjungu<u>n</u>utja*, 118–19.

41. See, for example, Congreve, "Investigations"; and Acker, *Somewhere in the World*; comments in Myers, "The Work of Art."

42. When Wartuma Tjungurrayi and Uta Uta Tjangala spoke to Myers in 1973,

they made clear some of the stakes: that the paintings were their stories, from their fathers and grandfathers, from and about their country; that they were concerned whitefellas might steal them; that they wanted to be compensated for them; and that the paintings expressed their hope to go back to their own country and to get a windmill there. Cited in Myers, *Painting Culture*, 25. See also Myers, "'We're Saving a Way of Life.'"

43. The Purple Truck dialysis unit is discussed in Paul Sweeney, "Art of Resilience," in Myers and Skerritt, *Irriṯitja Kuwarri Tjungu*, 89.

44. Crocker-curated exhibitions included *Mr. Sandman Bring Me a Dream* and a one-man show, *Charlie Tjaruru Tjungurrayi: A Retrospective 1970–1986*. See Crocker, *Mr. Sandman Bring Me a Dream*, 10; Tjungurrayi and Crocker, *Charlie Tjaruru Tjungurrayi*.

45. Scholl, "Preface," 9.

46. On this general question, see Smith, "Country, Indigeneity, Sovereignty." For an approach to the matter of Indigenous abstraction and its differences from abstract painting in the Western modernist tradition, see Smith, "Kngwarreye Woman Abstract Painter."

47. The others were Wartuma (Charlie Tarawa/Tjaruru) Tjungurrayi, *Moon Love Dreaming of Man and Woman—Medicine Story* (1971); John Scobie Tjapanangka, *Pintupi Women's Bush Tucker Dreaming* (1972); Shorty Lungkarta Tjungurrayi, *Mystery Sand Mosaic* (1974); Clifford Possum Tjapaltjarri, *Dreaming Story at Warlugulong* (1976); and Willy Tjungurrayi, *Pulpayella* (1976).

Chapter One. The Eternal Recurrence of Origins

1. Cited in Benjamin, *Icons of the Desert*, 79.

2. By this, Bardon meant that it showed "no more than the elements and the coefficients of a story and [required] no ornamentation." A similar work from this time, *Stars at Night*, by Old Walter Tjampitjinpa, is praised as "a valid simplification of a perceived object, an image for a star, in fact, an observed twinkling star." See Bardon and Bardon, *Papunya*, 106 and 105, respectively.

3. Bardon and Bardon, *Papunya*, 106; Johnson, *Once Upon a Time at Papunya*, color section.

4. Johnson, *Lives of the Papunya Tula Artists*, 58.

5. It is instructive to compare the dynamism of this painting to the one other known work by Kingsley Tjungurrayi, his *Water Dreaming*, also painted in 1971, using synthetic polymer powder paint on scrap wood. It exhibits a straightforward composition, with three vertical bands of conventional signs (flowing water and ceremonial objects with water designs), each different yet complementing each other, and three lines at one end ruling it off. Bardon's comment seems apt: "The simplicity of the patterning marks this painting as an archetypical example of its subject when technique and European materials were rudimentary." Bardon and Bardon, *Papunya*, 170. This was the mindset with which we

approached *Stars, Rain, and Lightning at Night*, only to discover a greater flexibility within it. There are close parallels to a painting by Wartuma (Charlie Tawara/Tjaruru) Tjungurrayi at the same time: *Rain, Hail, and Lightning Dreaming at Waterhole (Version 1)* in 1971. See Bardon and Bardon, *Papunya*, 174.

Chapter Two. The Ceremony Is the Place

1. See fig. 5.2. The journalist Michael Jensen's photographs, taken at Papunya in the Men's Painting Room during the winter of 1972, were rediscovered and published in the catalog for *Icons of the Desert* (14–21). They show the painters at work, sitting with each other in the Great Painting Room (as Bardon named it), the work they are doing, and some of the many finished works propped up in the background.

2. Benjamin, *Icons of the Desert*, 37, 123.

3. Kimber in Sotheby's, *Important Aboriginal Art*, 21. Kimber is one of the exceptionally knowledgeable non-Indigenous commentators on Papunya Tula Artists, a longtime local historian in Alice Springs, a one-time manager of Papunya Tula Artists, and a trusted recorder of sites for the Sacred Sites Authority in the Northern Territory.

4. Shorty's travels are extensively documented in Myers, *Pintupi Country*, 88.

5. This was Myers's response to Stephen Gilchrist's idea in his exhibition, *Everywhen*, to its insistence that we see past and present as equally implied in all Aboriginal artwork. See Myers, "Doublings."

6. Benjamin, *Icons of the Desert*, 123, citing Sotheby's, *Important Aboriginal Art*, 21. A soak or soakage is a source of water, common in Australian deserts, from water seeping or soaking into the ground and is stored below, available after digging below the surface. These are well known and named as places by the Indigenous inhabitants.

7. Kimber in Sotheby's, *Important Aboriginal Art*, 21.

8. Bardon and Bardon, *Papunya*, 200.

9. Bardon and Bardon, *Papunya*, 487.

10. See Warlukurlangu Artists, *Kuruwarri*; and Jones, *Behind the Doors*.

11. Illustrated in Bardon and Bardon, *Papunya*, 486.

12. Right next to his entries on these two paintings, Bardon says, "These works by Shorty Lungkarta were part of the programme direction that the men paint nonsecret material, the work of this time excluding ceremonial objects almost entirely but achieving an interesting visuality. Spatial constraints and the use of high-quality art materials with confidence by the painters were very important." Bardon and Bardon, *Papunya*, 487.

13. For reference to *chi chi tjuckatjuk*, see Bardon and Bardon, *Papunya*, 72. For the larger argument, see Skerritt, "Irriṯitja Kuwarri Tjungu," 11–13.

14. Kimber, "Politics of the Secret."

15. See Spencer and Gillen, *Native Tribes of Central Australia*, 305–11.

16. Myers, "Graceful Transfigurations."

17. Bardon and Bardon, *Papunya*, 486.

18. The same artist's *Goanna Love Story*, also painted in 1972 (presumably later in the year), uses a similar format to show the emergence of an ancestral goanna from its hole in the sandy desert and, in a striking single line that reaches to the lozenge shapes at the top and bottom, to track its movements "to find a wife." In his notes on this painting, Bardon expresses dismay that "this painting, while not secret, really was not a children's story." Bardon and Bardon, *Papunya*, 266.

Chapter Three. The Icy Spirit

1. The name "Charlie" seems to have come from his meeting with the South Australian doctor and ally of Aboriginal people Charles Duguid, in the mid-1930s at Hermannsburg. See Language and Person Names for further information.

2. Benjamin, *Icons of the Desert*, 133. See also Sotheby's, *Important Aboriginal Art*, 78.

3. Johnson, "The Intelligence of Pintupi Painting," 67. For his part, Roger Benjamin feels that the imagery supports Johnson's reading. See Benjamin, *Icons of the Desert*, 133.

4. See Ryan and Cooper, *Remembering Barak*.

5. Cited in Benjamin, *Icons of the Desert*, 165. Johnson discusses the multiple levels of meaning at work in this and other paintings by Wartuma, including their fictive and metaphorical levels, and comments on his distinctive sensibility in her essay "The Intelligence of Pintupi Painting." She notes that, at one time, he told her that the title of this painting was *Title*, which puns on the queen's power to confer titles, the inadequacy of many titles to paintings as summaries of their content, and, perhaps, the artificiality of the contemporary art-world practice of entitling paintings "Untitled." In the conclusion to his *Rattling Spears*, Ian McLean speculates that the painting might resonate something of the artist's experience when, six years earlier in Amsterdam, he participated in a performance piece by Ulay and Marina Abramović named *Nightsea Crossing Conjunction*. In this work, Wartuma, Buddhist monk Ngawang Soepa Lueyar, and the two artists sat at the cardinal points of a large circular table covered with twenty-four-karat gold for four days. McLean, *Rattling Spears*, 252–57. The spiritual telepathy hoped for by Ulay and Marina was not confirmed by Wartuma as having occurred on his part (remembered conversation with Fred Myers, date unknown).

6. Herman Melville, *Moby-Dick* (1851; Harmondsworth: Penguin, 2003), concluding paragraphs of chapter 42, "The Whiteness of the Whale."

Chapter Four. Inside and Outside

1. *Benny and the Dreamers*, dir. Ivo Burum (CAAMA Productions, 1992, 54 min.). Namarari is also considered in a full-length biography by Alec O'Halloran,

The Master from Marnpi, and an insightful essay by Philip Batty, "The Extraordinary Life and Times of Mick Namarari Tjapaltjarri."

2. The two earlier Pintupi films made by Sandall were *Pintubi Revisit Yumari* (1970) and *Pintubi Revisit Yaru Yaru* (1972). These films were made under the auspices of what was then the Australian Institute of Aboriginal Studies and later withdrawn from circulation because of emerging Indigenous concerns about the revelation of secret and sacred information. See Bryson, *Bringing to Light*.

3. The painting is illustrated, with detailed notes by Myers, in Benjamin, *Icons of the Desert*, 152–53. See Myers, "Graceful Transfigurations."

4. We will avoid the actual names given to these objects, in respect of the expectation of secrecy.

5. See Spencer and Gillen, *The Native Tribes of Central Australia*.

6. See, for example, the cover design for Mountford, *The Art of Albert Namatjira*.

7. See Bardon and Bardon, *Papunya*, 436, and the text online for this painting on the National Gallery of Victoria website at https://www.ngv.vic.gov.au/explore/collection/work/2313/. The painting was purchased in 1985 by Margaret Carnegie and her son from Bardon's collection and later acquired by the National Gallery of Victoria, at a then record price of AU$187,000, as a work to commemorate the bicentennial of the gallery. See J. Ryan, "The Quick and the Dead."

8. At issue is that actual ceremonies are reenactments of ancestral ceremonies that created the place, the landscape, whose activities left behind the features of the place. Conversely, places are themselves "records" or "signs" of ancestral activity and ancestral ceremony. By the time I (Myers) arrived at Yayayi, these developments had occurred, and all the paintings I saw were simultaneously of place and ceremony, in some fashion, with representation of sacred objects sometimes identified with what I would see in a ceremony and sometimes with a feature in the landscape. Of course, they were both.

9. See Róheim, *The Eternal Ones of the Dream*.

10. See Myers, *Pintupi Country, Pintupi Self*, 68–69; and Myers, "Showing Too Much or Too Little."

11. See *Man Corroboree* (1971–72), Kluge-Ruhe Collection of Australian Aboriginal Art, University of Virginia.

Chapter Five. Stippling Plenitude

1. Benjamin, *Icons of the Desert*, 127.

2. Kean, "East to West," 42.

3. Bullen et al., *John Mawurndjul*. See also the exhibition website *John Mawurndjul*: https://www.johnmawurndjul.com.

4. Morphy, "From Dull to Brilliant."

5. For an illustration, see Benjamin, *Icons of the Desert*, 108–9. A recently recovered painting by Kaapa, *Mikantji and Tywerle*, also sets ceremonial figures and

objects on a deep black background. It was one of the eight submitted for the Caltex Prize in Alice Springs in August 1971, of which Kaapa was the joint winner. It is illustrated in Kean, *Dot, Circle, and Frame*, as plate 28 and discussed by him in the catalog for the exhibition *Significant* (D'Lan Contemporary, Melbourne, Australia, June–July 2023).

6. Kean, *Dot, Circle, and Frame*, 252–59; Kimber, "The Artists' Country through Aboriginal Eyes," 44–46.

7. See Morphy, *Aboriginal Art*; and Lendon, "Innovation and Its Meanings."

8. Bardon and Bardon, *Papunya*, 158.

9. Several are illustrated in Bardon and Bardon, *Papunya*, 158–69.

10. Myers, "Doublings," note 10.

11. Bardon and Bardon, *Papunya*, 168.

12. Benjamin, *Icons of the Desert*, 85. The painting is illustrated in Bardon and Bardon, *Papunya*, 220, where the structure is characterized as a "radiating configuration."

13. Discussed in Kean, "East to West," 42–43. The painting is illustrated in Myers and Skerritt, *Irriṯitja Kuwarri Tjungu*, 112, plate 9.

Chapter Six. Dotting and Weaving

1. Benjamin, *Icons of the Desert*, discussion of paintings minus reproduction, 85 and 110–11, and Supplement 3 and 12.

2. See Benjamin, *Icons of the Desert*, 138–39. Another close parallel is *Honey Ant Dreaming*, 1972, in the Australian Museum, Sydney, variously attributed to either Tim Leura or Clifford Possum. See the discussion in Johnson, *Clifford Possum Tjapaltjarri*, 220–21.

3. Benjamin, *Icons of the Desert*, 141.

4. Yuendumu is/was another government-overseen settlement for Aboriginal people, ninety miles (155 kilometers) north of Papunya. Now an independent community, Yuendumu was home to people who were mostly Warlpiri-speaking. Elders of this community were active artists by the late 1960s. The Yuendumu Men's Museum, containing secret objects as well as recently painted murals, opened in July 1971. Access was initially restricted to initiated men and new initiates. It partly inspired developments at Papunya. See "Yuendumu Men's Museum," Warlukurlangu: Artists of Yuendumu, accessed January 25, 2024, https://warlu.com/community-projects/mens-museum/.

5. *Crotalaria cunninghamii*, also known as green birdflower, birdflower ratulpo, and parrot pea.

6. R. G. Kimber, "Relatives of the Artists Respond to the Paintings," in Benjamin, *Icons of the Desert*, 75. In Warlpiri, the word *ngalyipi* refers to the Ramsay's woma python (*Aspidites ramsayi*), a short and squat python of the area.

7. See John Kean on Warangkula's influence on Tim Leura's color preferences, in Kean, *Dot, Circle, and Frame*, 266 and 270.

8. John Kean advises that the plural in the title is misleading, as this is clearly one snake whose activities are mirrored according to the symmetrical template in use in this as in so many other paintings of the period and since. He identifies the snake as Jarapiri, an inland taipan. Personal communication with Myers, February 5, 2023. In 1978, this painting was woven into a tapestry by the Victorian Tapestry Workshop, which is now in the collection of the Victorian Arts Centre, Southbank, Melbourne. See "Winparrku Serpents, The," Arts Centre Melbourne, accessed January 25, 2024, https://collections.artscentremelbourne.com.au/#details=ecatalogue.5000235.

9. Sotheby's Australia auction, June 2002, catalog entry 74. The work is synthetic polymer powder paint on composition board, 78 × 45.5 cm.

10. A large circular band marks out the borders of a ceremonial ground in other paintings from the period; for example, *Love Story*, 1972, in the collection of the National Gallery of Australia, Canberra. See "Love Story," National Gallery of Australia, accessed January 25, 2024, https://searchthecollection.nga.gov.au/object/250860.

11. Myers, "Doublings," 38–39.

12. Myers, "Doublings," 42.

13. Myers, "Doublings," 42.

14. The two earlier paintings Clifford Possum produced in the Men's Painting Room were *Emu Corroboree Man* (1972) (see comment in text) and *Love Story* (1972). The latter painting vividly suggests its narrative through an innovative disposition of implements used by the ancestral man Liltipililti to attract the Napangati women to his campsite, but without depicting him as a figure. We see this as a step toward the further abstraction of an event arrived at in *Honey Ant Ceremony*. See the discussion of these paintings in Johnson, *Clifford Possum Tjapaltjarri*, 64, 219–20.

15. These two drawings were confined, unattributed, in the T. G. H. Strehlow collection at the Museum of South Australia for many years. As mentioned in the introduction, John Kean attributes them to Namatjira on entirely plausible grounds and points out the close correspondences to the schema of *Honey Ant Ceremony*. See his discussion in *Dot, Circle, and Frame* on pages 45–47. On page 44 he illustrates a 1940 photograph by Charles Mountford of Namatjira, drawing, with crayon, his family group totem in a similar fashion.

16. Kaapa Mbitjana Tjampitjinpa, *Untitled* (1971), synthetic polymer paint on composition board, Art Gallery of South Australia, A. R. and A. M. Ragless Bequest 1989, 8911P33.

17. Vivien Johnson suggests that it is "Yuulkuru, or more likely, Yinyalingi, where, in mythological times, groups of Honey Ant people gathered for men's and women's ceremonies," a site often painted by the artist. See Johnson, *Clifford Possum Tjapaltjarri*, 220. On the twinned states of being and the importance of the Honey Ant Dreaming for the Aranda/Anmatyerr, see Strehlow, "Personal Monotheism."

18. Bardon and Bardon, *Papunya*, 333.

19. Johnson, *Clifford Possum Tjapaltjarri*, 220.

20. Specifically, Tim Leura's *Honey Ant Ancestors* (1974). See Kean, *Dot, Circle, and Frame*, 269–70.

21. *Two Snakes at Alinitti* was painted in 1972 using synthetic powder paint, dimensions 92 × 67 cm. It was exhibited and sold at Sotheby's, Melbourne, in the Aboriginal Art sale of June 26, 2000, lot 111. No further information is archived at the successor company, Smith & Singer, nor is there a publishable reproduction. An image is available online at https://in.pinterest.com/pin/374572894002674946/.

22. More of the story is revealed in *Two Snakes at Alinitti* than in the shield painting. Bardon's notations suggest that the central band, so fiercely horizontal, shows the snakes swirling their way through the waterhole and out the other side. Above and below, in close symmetry, are the smaller waterholes, formed by droplets falling from the snakes as they traveled. Bardon and Bardon, *Papunya*, 236. Kean identifies them as a pair of black-headed pythons that move through Lake Lewis north of Papunya and then head west, one of them becoming another snake. Clifford Possum painted them often, sometimes referring to them as "rainbow snakes." Personal communication with Myers, February 5, 2023.

23. Bardon's notes on this painting point us toward Kaapa's *Sandhill Dancing (Version 1)*, a relatively straightforward notation of "a very big dancing ceremony," painted six months or so earlier, in which the main journey of ancestral beings (unspecified, perhaps snakes, but again which ones remain unspecified) across sandhills is shown through the central register, while the journeys of two sets of men who celebrate their passage by dancing alongside them are shown as parallel lines of smaller looping forms. See Bardon and Bardon, *Papunya*, 117.

24. Also known as *Bush Fire Dreaming*. See Benjamin, *Icons of the Desert*, 146–47. Earlier in the year, Clifford Possum painted the Honey Ant theme using atmospheric overlays that Bardon reads as "rigorously desacralized" in intent. See Bardon and Bardon, *Papunya*, 332, 333. The white-over-black hatching and atmospheric overlays are also used in the artist's *Man's Love Story*, painted the following year, two versions of which are illustrated in Bardon and Bardon, *Papunya*, 265, 266. The first is in the collection of the Art Gallery of South Australia.

25. See Smith, "The Painting of David Aspden," 50–53, 79.

26. Two previous instances of the inclusion of single works in such surveys are known. In 1978 Murphy included a Papunya painting in *Landscape and Image*, which toured Indonesia in 1978. And curator Ron Radford hung Clifford Possum Tjapaltjarri's *Man's Love Story* in the contemporary Australian art rooms of the Art Gallery of South Australia in 1980.

27. Benjamin, *Icons of the Desert*, 141.

28. In his chapter about "The Great Painting Room" Bardon cites this painting as an example of what he was told was a "dangerous" (*maku*) subject, and notes having been told that this snake variety was "a small snake the size of a finger and

had wings." Bardon and Bardon, *Papunya*, 31. The variety of snake species and their many roles within the Dreaming require further inquiry and consultation with community members.

A Reflection

1. Benjamin, *Icons of the Desert*, 21.
2. Simpson and Smith, "Introduction," 7.
3. Djon Mundine, "Djon Mundine on 21 Years of Aboriginal Art," *Awaye!, Radio National*, accessed April 18, 2019, https://www.abc.net.au/radionational/programs/awaye/djon-mundine-21-years-of-aboriginal-art/4881588.
4. Myers, "Beyond the Intentional Fallacy," 11.
5. Thomas, "Beginnings," 17.
6. Smith, "Currents of World-Making," 174.

Glossary

1. Myers, *Pintupi Country, Pintupi Self*, 61.
2. Stanner, "The Dreaming," 27.
3. Stanner, "The Dreaming," 29.
4. Myers, *Pintupi Country, Pintupi Self*, 49.

Bibliography

Acker, Tim. *Somewhere in the World: Aboriginal and Torres Strait Islander Art and Its Place in the Global Art Market*. Alice Springs: Ninti One Limited, 2016.

Anderson, Christopher, and Françoise Dussart. "Dreamings in Acrylic: Western Desert Art." In *Dreamings: The Art of Aboriginal Australia*, edited by Peter Sutton, 89–142. New York: George Braziller, 1988.

Bardon, Geoffrey. *Aboriginal Art of the Western Desert*. Adelaide: Rigby, 1979.

Bardon, Geoffrey. *Papunya Tula: Art of the Western Desert*. Ringwood: McPhee Gribble, 1991.

Bardon, Geoffrey, and James Bardon. *Papunya: A Place Made after the Story: The Beginnings of the Western Desert Painting Movement*. Melbourne: Miegunyah Press, 2004.

Batty, Philip. "The Extraordinary Life and Times of Mick Namarari Tjapaltjarri: Warrior, Stockman, Artist." In *Papunya Painting: Out of the Desert*, edited by Vivien Johnson, 16–26. Canberra: National Museum of Australia Press, 2007.

Benjamin, Roger. "The Fetish for Papunya Boards." In *Icons of the Desert: Early Aboriginal Paintings from Papunya*, edited by Roger Benjamin, 21–49. Ithaca, NY: Herbert F. Johnson Museum of Art, Cornell University, 2009.

Benjamin, Roger, with Andrew C. Weislogel, eds. *Icons of the Desert: Early Aboriginal Paintings from Papunya*. Ithaca, NY: Herbert F. Johnson Museum of Art, Cornell University, 2009.

Biddle, Jennifer Loureide. *Breasts, Bodies, Canvas: Central Desert Art as Experience*. Sydney: University of New South Wales Press, 2007.

Biddle, Jennifer Loureide. *Remote Avant-Garde: Aboriginal Art under Occupation*. Durham, NC: Duke University Press, 2016.

Brody, Annemarie. *The Face of the Centre: Papunya Tula Paintings 1971–1984*. Melbourne: National Gallery of Victoria, 1985.

Brooks, David, and Darren Jorgensen. *Wanarn Painters of Place and Time: Old Age Travels in the Tjukurrpa*. Crawley: University of Western Australia Press, 2015.

Bryson, Ian. *Bringing to Light: A History of Ethnographic Filmmaking at the Australian Institute of Aboriginal and Torres Strait Islander Studies*. Canberra: Aboriginal Studies Press, 2002.

Bullen, Clothilde, et al. *John Mawurndjul: I Am the Old and the New*. Sydney: Museum of Contemporary Art Australia, 2003.

Burn, Ian, and Ann Stephen. "Namatjira's White Mask: A Partial Interpretation." In *The Heritage of Namatjira*, edited by Jane Hardy, J. V. S. Megaw, and M. Ruth Megaw, 249–83. Melbourne: William Heinemann, 1992.

Carter, Paul. "Introduction: The Interpretation of Dreams." In *Papunya: A Place Made after the Story: The Beginnings of the Western Desert Painting Movement*, edited by Geoffrey Bardon and James Bardon, xiv–xxi. Melbourne: Miegunyah Press, 2004.

Carty, John. *Balgo: Creating Country*. Crawley: Western Australia Press, 2021.

Carty, John. "The Limits of Criticism." *Artlink* 33, no. 2 (2013): 56–61.

Carty, John, and Alison French. "Art of Central Australia: Refigured Ground." In *The Cambridge Companion to Australian Art*, edited by Jaynie Anderson, 122–42. Melbourne: Cambridge University Press, 2011.

Caruana, Wally. *Aboriginal Art*. London: Thames and Hudson, 1993.

Clifford, James. *The Predicament of Culture*. Cambridge, MA: Harvard University Press, 1988.

Congreve, Susan. "Investigations into the Role of the Enabling Environment in Supporting Indigenous Economic Development: A Case Study of Remote Community Aboriginal and Torres Strait Islander Art Centres 2007–2013." PhD thesis, Curtin University, Western Australia, 2016.

Crocker, Andrew. *Mr. Sandman Bring Me a Dream*. Sydney: Papunya Tula and Aboriginal Artists Agency, 1981.

Dussart, Françoise. "A Body Painting in Translation." In *Rethinking Visual Anthropology*, edited by Marcus Banks and Howard Morphy, 186–202. New Haven, CT: Yale University Press, 1997.

Dussart, Françoise. "Canvassing Identities: Reflecting on the Acrylic Art Movement in an Australian Aboriginal Settlement." *Aboriginal History* 30 (2006): 156–68.

Edmond, Martin. *Battarbee and Namatjira*. Artarmon, NSW: Giramondo, 2014.

Fordham, Douglas, and Ash Duhrkoop, eds. *Boomalli Prints and Paper: Making Space as an Art Collective*. Charlottesville: Kluge-Ruhe Aboriginal Art Collection, University of Virginia, 2022.

French, Alison. *Seeing the Centre: The Art of Albert Namatjira 1902–1959*. Canberra: National Gallery of Australia, 2002.

Gilchrist, Stephen, ed. *Everywhen: The Eternal Present in Indigenous Art from Australia*. New Haven, CT: Yale University Press, 2016.

Gilchrist, Stephen. "Indigenous Curatorial Interpellations: Insistence and Refusal." In *The Australian Art Field: Practices, Policies, Institutions*, edited

by Tony Bennett, Deborah Stevenson, Fred Myers, and Tamara Winikoff, 252–65. London: Routledge, 2020.
Graburn, Nelson, ed. *Ethnic and Tourist Arts: Cultural Expression from the Fourth World*. Berkeley: University of California Press, 1976.
Hogan, Pat. "Notes and Inventory for the Early Consignments of Pintupi Paintings." In *Dot and Circle: A Retrospective Survey of the Aboriginal Acrylic Paintings of Central Australia*, edited by J. Megaw, J. Maughan, and J. Zimmer, 45–49, 55–57. Melbourne: Royal Melbourne Institute of Technology, 1986.
Jack-Hinton, Colin. *Aboriginal Art Past and Present*. Darwin: Government Printer, 1980.
Johnson, Vivien. *Aboriginal Artists of the Western Desert: A Biographical Dictionary*. Roseville East: Craftsman House, 1994.
Johnson, Vivien. *The Art of Clifford Possum Tjapaltjarri*. Roseville East: Gordon and Beach International, 1994.
Johnson, Vivien. *The Art of Michael Nelson Jagamara*. Sydney: Craftsman House, 1997.
Johnson, Vivien. *Clifford Possum Tjapaltjarri*. Adelaide: Art Gallery of South Australia, 2003.
Johnson, Vivien. "The Intelligence of Pintupi Painting." In *Icons of the Desert: Early Aboriginal Painting from Papunya*, edited by Roger Benjamin, 65–70. Ithaca, NY: Herbert F. Johnson Museum of Art, Cornell University, 2009.
Johnson, Vivien. *Lives of the Papunya Tula Artists*. Alice Springs: IAD Press, 2008.
Johnson, Vivien. *Once Upon a Time in Papunya*. Sydney: University of New South Wales Press, 2010.
Johnson, Vivien, ed. *Papunya Painting: Out of the Desert*. Canberra: National Museum of Australia Press, 2007.
Jones, Philip. *Behind the Doors: An Art History from Yuendumu*. Adelaide: Wakefield Press, 2014.
Jorgensen, Darren. "New Histories of the Papunya Boards, New Beginnings for the Western Desert Painting Movement." *Art Bulletin* 105, no. 2 (July 2023): 7–35.
Kean, John. "Digging for Honey Ants: Revisiting the Papunya Mural Project." *Index*, no. 4, November 20, 2020. https://index-journal.org/issues/monument/digging-for-honey-ants-revisiting-the-papunya-mural-project.
Kean, John. "Dot, Circle, and Frame: How Kaapa Tjampitjinpa, Tim Leura, Clifford Possum and Johnny Warangula Created Papunya Art." PhD diss., University of Melbourne, 2020.
Kean, John. *Dot, Circle, and Frame: The Making of Papunya Tula Art*. Perth: Upswell Publishing, 2023.
Kean, John. "East to West: The Diversity of Papunya Art." In *Irriṯitja Kuwarri Tjungu / Past and Present Together: Fifty Years of Papunya Tula Artists*, edited by Fred Myers and Henry Skerritt, 39–49. Charlottesville: University of Virginia Press, 2021.

Kean, John. “Framing Papunya Painting: Form, Style and Representation, 1971–72.” In *Tjungunutja: From Having Come Together*, edited by Luke Scholes, 172–95. Darwin: Museum and Art Gallery of the Northern Territory, 2017.

Kean, John. “Papunya: Place and Time.” In *Papunya Painting: Out of the Desert*, edited by Vivien Johnson, 5–15. Canberra: National Museum of Australia Press, 2007.

Kimber, R. G. (Dick). “The Artists’ Country through Aboriginal Eyes.” In *Wildbird Dreaming: Aboriginal Art from the Central Deserts of Australia*, edited by Nadine Amadio and R. G. Kimber, 44–46. Melbourne: Greenhouse, 1988.

Kimber, R. G. (Dick). “Politics of the Secret in Contemporary Western Desert Art.” In *Politics of the Secret*, edited by Christopher Anderson, 123–42. Sydney: Oceania, 1995.

Lendon, Nigel. “Innovation and Its Meanings.” In *No Ordinary Place: The Art of David Malangi*, edited by Susan Jenkins, 53–58. Canberra: National Gallery of Australia, 2004.

McGregor, Ken. *The Life and Times of Albert Namatjira*. Melbourne: Badger Editions, 2021.

McLean, Ian, ed. *How Aborigines Invented the Idea of Contemporary Art*. Brisbane: Institute of Modern Art / Sydney: Power Institute Publications, 2010.

McLean, Ian. *Rattling Spears: A History of Indigenous Australia Art*. London: Reaktion, 2016.

Megaw, J. V. S., Janet Maughan, and Jenny Zimmer, eds. *Dot and Circle: A Retrospective Survey of the Aboriginal Acrylic Paintings of Central Australia*. Melbourne: Royal Melbourne Institute of Technology, 1986.

Morphy, Howard. *Aboriginal Art*. London: Phaidon, 1998.

Morphy, Howard. *Ancestral Connections: Art and an Aboriginal System of Knowledge*. Chicago: University of Chicago Press, 1991.

Morphy, Howard. *Becoming Art: Exploring Cross-Cultural Categories*. Sydney: University of New South Wales Press, 2008.

Morphy, Howard. “From Dull to Brilliant: The Aesthetics of Spiritual Power among the Yolngu.” *Man* 24 (1989): 21–40.

Mountford, Charles Pearcy. *The Art of Albert Namatjira*. Melbourne: Bread and Cheese Club, 1951.

Munn, Nancy D. “Visual Categories: An Approach to the Study of Representational Systems.” *American Anthropologist* 68, no. 4 (1966): 936–50.

Munn, Nancy D. “Walbiri Graphic Signs: An Analysis.” *American Anthropologist* 64, no. 5 (1962): 972–84.

Munn, Nancy D. *Walbiri Iconography: Graphic Symbolism and Cultural Representation in a Central Australian Society*. Ithaca, NY: Cornell University Press, 1993.

Myers, Fred. “Beyond the Intentional Fallacy: Art Criticism and the Ethnography of Aboriginal Acrylic Painting.” *Visual Anthropology Review* 10, no. 1 (1994): 10–43.

Myers, Fred. "Doublings." In *Everywhen: The Eternal Present in Indigenous Art from Australia*, edited by Stephen Gilchrist, 36–43. New Haven, CT: Yale University Press, 2016.
Myers, Fred. "Graceful Transfigurations of Person, Place and Story: The Stylistic Evolution of Shorty Lungkarta Tjungurrayi." In *Icons of the Desert: Early Aboriginal Paintings from Papunya*, edited by Roger Benjamin, 51–64. Ithaca, NY: Herbert F. Johnson Museum of Art, Cornell University, 2009.
Myers, Fred. *Painting Culture: The Making of an Aboriginal High Art*. Durham, NC: Duke University Press, 2002.
Myers, Fred. "Paintings, Publics and Protocols: The Early Paintings from Papunya." *Material Culture Review / Revue de la Culture Materielle* 79 (Spring 2015): 78–91.
Myers, Fred. *Pintupi Country, Pintupi Self: Sentiment, Place, and Politics among Western Desert Aborigines*. Washington, DC: Smithsonian Institution Press, 1986.
Myers, Fred. "Showing Too Much or Too Little: Predicaments of Painting Indigenous Presence in Central Australia." In *Performing Indigeneity*, edited by Glenn Penny and Laura Graham, 351–89. Lincoln: University of Nebraska Press, 2014.
Myers, Fred. "Traffic in Culture: On Knowing Pintupi Painting." In *Impossible Presence: Surface and Screen in the Photogenic Era*, edited by Terry Smith, 237–84. Sydney: Power Institute Publications / Chicago: University of Chicago Press, 2001.
Myers, Fred. "'We're Saving a Way of Life': Indigenous Australian Acrylic Painting and Its Troubles with the Categories of Art and Value." In *The Trouble with Art*, edited by Roger Sansi and Jonas Tinius. London: Routledge, 2024.
Myers, Fred. "The Work of Art: Hope, Disenchantment and Indigenous Art in Australia." In *The Australian Art Field: Practices, Policies, Institutions*, edited by Tony Bennett, Deborah Stevenson, Fred Myers, and Tamara Winikoff, 209–21. London: Routledge, 2020.
Myers, Fred, and Henry Skerritt, eds. *Irriṯitja Kuwarri Tjungu / Past and Present Together: Fifty Years of Papunya Tula Artists*. Charlottesville: University of Virginia Press, 2021.
O'Halloran, Alec B. *The Master from Marnpi: Mick Namarari Tjapaltjarri*. Sydney: LifeDesign Australia, 2018.
Perkins, Hetti. "Stories I Can Tell: Hetti Perkins in Conversation with Fred Myers and Henry Skerritt." In *Irriṯitja Kuwarri Tjungu / Past and Present Together: Fifty Years of Papunya Tula Artists*, edited by Fred Myers and Henry Skerritt, 74–83. Charlottesville: University of Virginia Press, 2021.
Perkins, Hetti, and Hannah Fink, eds. *Papunya Tula: Genesis and Genius*. Sydney: Art Gallery of New South Wales, 2000.
Phillips, Ruth B., and Norman Vorano, eds. *Mediating Modernisms: Indigenous Artists, Modernist Mediators, Global Networks*. Durham, NC: Duke University Press, forthcoming.

Rey, Una. "Bardon's Legacy: Paintings, Stories, and Indigenous Australian Art." In *Mediating Modernisms: Indigenous Artists, Modernist Mediators, Global Networks*, edited by Ruth B. Phillips and Norman Vorano. Durham, NC: Duke University Press, forthcoming.

Róheim, Géza. *The Eternal Ones of the Dream: A Psychoanalytic Interpretation of Australian Myth and Ritual.* New York: International Universities Press, 1945.

Ryan, Allan J. *The Trickster Shift: Humour and Irony in Contemporary Native Art.* Vancouver: University of British Columbia Press / Seattle: University of Washington Press, 1999.

Ryan, Judith. *Mythscapes: Aboriginal Art of the Desert from the National Gallery of Victoria.* Melbourne: National Gallery of Victoria, 1989.

Ryan, Judith. "The Quick and the Dead, Purchasing Indigenous Art 1988–1990." *Art Bulletin of Victoria, National Gallery of Victoria*, no. 44 (2004): 70–81. https://www.ngv.vic.gov.au/essay/the-quick-and-the-dead-purchasing-indigenous-art-1988-1990/.

Ryan, Judith, and Philip Batty, eds. *Tjukurrtjanu: Origins of Western Desert Art.* Melbourne: National Gallery of Victoria, 2011.

Ryan, Judith, and Carol Cooper. *Remembering Barak.* Melbourne: National Gallery of Victoria, 2003.

Scholes, Luke, ed. *Tjungu̲nutja: From Having Come Together.* Darwin: Museum and Art Gallery of the Northern Territory, 2017.

Scholes, Luke. "Unmasking the Myth: The Emergence of Papunya Painting." In *Tjungu̲nutja: From Having Come Together*, edited by Luke Scholes, 126–61. Darwin: Museum and Art Gallery of the Northern Territory, 2017.

Scholl, Dennis. "Preface." In *No Boundaries: Aboriginal Australian Contemporary Abstract Painting from the Debra and Dennis Scholl Collection*, edited by Henry Skerritt. Munich: Prestel for the Nevada Museum of Art, 2014.

Simpson, Audra, and Andrea Smith. "Introduction." In *Theorizing Native Studies*, edited by Audra Simpson and Andrea Smith, 1–30. Durham, NC: Duke University Press, 2014.

Skerritt, Henry. "Irri̲titja Kuwarri Tjungu—Past and Present Together." In *Irri̲titja Kuwarri Tjungu / Past and Present Together: Fifty Years of Papunya Tula Artists*, edited by Fred Myers and Henry Skerritt, 1–21. Charlottesville: University of Virginia Press, 2021.

Skerritt, Henry, ed. *No Boundaries: Aboriginal Australian Contemporary Abstract Painting from the Debra and Dennis Scholl Collection.* Munich: Prestel for the Nevada Museum of Art, 2014.

Smith, Terry. "Albert Namatjira and Margaret Preston: Changing an Unequal Exchange." In *Transformations in Australian Art*, vol. 2: *The Twentieth Century—Modernism and Aboriginality*, 74–91. Sydney: Craftsman House, 2002.

Smith, Terry. "Country, Indigeneity, Sovereignty." In *Art to Come: Histories of Contemporary Art*, 156–97. Durham, NC: Duke University Press, 2019.

Smith, Terry. "Currents of World-Making in Contemporary Art." *World Art* 1, no. 2 (2011): 20–36.
Smith, Terry. "From the Desert: Aboriginal Painting 1970–1990." In *Australian Painting 1788–1990*, by Bernard Smith with Terry Smith, 495–517. Melbourne: Oxford University Press, 1991.
Smith, Terry. "Kngwarreye Woman Abstract Painter." In *Emily Kngwarreye Paintings*, edited by Jennifer Isaacs, 24–42. Sydney: Craftsman House, 1998.
Smith, Terry. "The Painting of David Aspden." *Art International* 14, no. 8 (1970): 50–53, 79.
Sotheby's. *Important Aboriginal Art*. Melbourne, June 30, 1997.
Spencer, Baldwin, and F. J. Gillen. *The Native Tribes of Central Australia*. London: Macmillan, 1899.
Sprague, Quentin. *The Stranger Artist: Life at the Edge of Kimberley Painting*. Melbourne: Hardie Grant Books, 2020.
Sprague, Quentin. "White Privilege and Black Disadvantage in the Aboriginal Art Industry." *The Monthly*, April 21, 2023, https://www.themonthly.com.au/blog/quentin-sprague/2023/21/2023/white-privilege-and-black-disadvantage-aboriginal-art-industry.
Stanner, W. E. H. "The Dreaming." In *White Man Got No Dreaming: Essays 1938–1973*, 23–40. Canberra: Australian National University Press, 1979.
Strehlow, T. G. H. "Personal Monotheism in a Polytotemic Community." 1964. Republished as *Central Australian Religion*. Bedford Park: Australian Association for the Study of Religion, 1978.
Sutton, Peter, ed. *Dreamings: The Art of Aboriginal Australia*. New York: George Braziller, 1988.
Sutton, Peter. "The Morphology of Feeling." In *Dreamings: The Art of Aboriginal Australia*, edited by Peter Sutton, 59–88. New York: George Braziller, 1988.
Sutton, Peter. *The Politics of Suffering: Indigenous Australia and the End of the Liberal Consensus*. Melbourne: Melbourne University Press, 2009.
Thomas, Nicholas. "Beginnings." In *Possessions: Indigenous Art / Colonial Culture*, 24–70. London: Thames and Hudson, 1999.
Tjungurrayi, Charlie Tjaruru, and Andrew Crocker. *Charlie Tjaruru Tjungurrayi: A Retrospective 1970–1986*. Orange, NSW: Orange City Council, 1987.
Warlukurlangu Artists. *Kuruwarri*. Canberra: Australian Institute of Aboriginal Studies, 1987.
Watson, Christine. "Touching the Land: Towards an Aesthetic of Balgo Contemporary Painting." In *Art from the Land: Dialogues with the Kluge-Ruhe Collection of Australian Aboriginal Art*, edited by Howard Morphy and Margo Smith Boles, 163–92. Seattle: University of Washington Press, 1999.
Williamson, Stephen. *Unique Perspectives: Papunya Tula Artists and the Alice Springs Community*. Alice Springs: Araluen Art Centre and Papunya Tula Artists, 2012.

Index

Aboriginal art. *See* Indigenous art
Aboriginal Art of the Western Desert (Bardon), 11
Abramović, Marina, 102n5
abstractionism: contemporary abstract painting, 81; Indigenous abstraction versus, 22–23, 59–60, 100n46; modernism and, 21–22; in Western Desert art, 18, 21–23, 59, 79, 105n14. *See also* doubling (aesthetics of); modernism; veiling (practice of); Western Desert art
Acker, Tim, 99n41
agency, 11–18, 86, 88–90, 98n9
Alice Springs (place), 6, 8, 21, 40, 56, 62, 64, 75, 85, 101n3, 103–4n5
Anderson, Sid, 16
Anmatyerr, 7, 15–16, 23, 59, 65, 77–78, 91, 105n17
anthropology: approaches to Indigenous art, 6; art history and, 2, 86–89; colonialism in, 2, 86–89; curating as a practice of, 3; history in relation to Indigenous peoples, 3, 49, 52, 85, 94, 97n2, 98n20; Indigenous theorizing in, 86–87; methods and, 2, 10, 85–88. *See also* multidisciplinarity
Arrernte, 4, 7, 23, 49, 91
art exhibitions. See *Australian Perspecta*; *Everywhen*; *Icons of the Desert*; Indigenous art; *Papunya Tula: Genesis and Genius*; *Tjungunutja, from having come together*; Western Desert art
art galleries. *See* Art Gallery of New South Wales (Sydney); Art Gallery of South Australia (Adelaide); Grey Art Gallery (New York); Museum and Art Gallery of the Northern Territory (Darwin); National Gallery of Australia (Canberra); National Gallery of Victoria (Melbourne)
Art Gallery of New South Wales (Sydney), 4–5, 43, 81–82
Art Gallery of South Australia (Adelaide), 58, 75–76, 99n31, 105n16, 106n24, 106n26
art history and criticism, 37; anthropology and, 2, 86–89; commodification of culture, 6, 17–18; curating as a practice of, 3; hierarchies in, 2, 30, 81, 85–89, 98n17; impact of Indigenous art on, 15–18, 22, 81, 86–89; Indigenous values in, 3, 18, 85, 87–89; methods of, 3, 14, 87–89; theft and co-optation in, 88, 99–100n42. *See also* abstractionism; Indigenous art; modernism; multidisciplinarity
art materials, 4, 22, 29, 37, 59, 64, 70, 79, 86, 101n12. *See also* Western Desert art
Aspden, David, 81
assimilation policy, 6–7, 15, 17–18, 104n4. *See also* displacement
Audience with the Queen (Wartuma Tjungurrayi), 44–45
Australian Indigenous art. *See* Indigenous art; Western Desert art

Australian Museum (Sydney), 104n2
Australian Perspecta (exhibition), 81

Barak, William, 42
Bardon, Geoffrey: annotations of, 23, 30–31, 33–37, 49, 52, 61, 77–78, 100–101n5, 106nn22–24; art collection of, 103n7; attitude toward secret knowledge, 75, 101n12, 102n18, 106–7n28; filmmaking, 47, 50; Nancy Munn and, 98n20; relationship with Papunya Tula artists, 7, 11–14, 16, 21–22, 29, 56, 63, 101n1; successor of, 98n17. *See also* Papunya School
Bardon, James, 11
Battarbee, Rex, 14
Batty, Philip, 102–3n1
Benjamin, Roger, 9, 30, 44, 55, 85, 102n2, 102n5, 106n24
Benny and the Dreamers (film), 47
Big Cave Dreaming with Ceremonial Objects (Mick Namarari Tjapaltjarri), 46–53
Big Family Kangaroo Ceremonial Dreaming (Long Jack Phillipus Tjakamarra), 63–64
Big Red (Aspden), 81
body painting, 16, 23, 25–26, 30–31, 34, 37, 43, 97n2. *See also* ground painting
Boomalli Aboriginal Artists' Cooperative, 99
Brooks, David, 97n2
Bryson, Ian, 103n2
Budgerigar Dreaming (Version 1) (Kaapa Mbitjana Tjampitjinpa), 67
Burn, Ian, 99n30
Bushfire Spirit Dreaming at Napperby (Tim Leura Tjapaltjarri), 68–69

Caltex Prize (Northern Territory Art Award), 62, 75, 104n5
Carnegie, Margaret, 103n7
Carter, Paul, 12
Carty, John, 97n2
Central Australian movement, 15, 97n2. *See also* Western Desert art
ceremony. *See* body painting; geographies (sacred); ground painting; sacredness and protocols
Children's Water Dreaming (Version 2) (Shorty Lungkarta Tjungurrayi), 10, 32–33, 37, 74
Classic Pintupi Water Dreaming (Shorty Lungkarta Tjungurrayi), 10, 28–37, 41, 58
Clifford, James, 97n1
Congreve, Susan, 99n41
contemporary art: association with Land Rights, 15; Indigenous art and, 1, 5, 15–19, 22, 81, 87–88, 102n5, 106n26; tradition and, 13–14, 18. *See also* abstractionism; modernism; Western Desert art
Crocker, Andrew, 13, 18, 100n44
Croft, Brenda L., 3, 97n4

de Kooning, Willem, 79
disciplinary methods. *See* multidisciplinarity
displacement, 7, 15–17, 48, 62, 100n42. *See also* assimilation policy
doubling (aesthetics of), 30, 56, 62, 73–75, 77
Dreaming Story at Warlugulong (Clifford Possum Tjapaltjarri), 100n47
Duguid, Charles, 91, 102n1
Duhrkoop, Ash, 99n25

Edmond, Martin, 99n29
Emu Corroboree Man (Clifford Possum Tjapaltjarri), 59, 77, 105n14
Everywhen (exhibition), 73, 97, 101n5
exile. *See* displacement

Family Bush Tucker Dreaming (Mick Namarari Tjapaltjarri), 35
Fannin, Peter, 13, 68–69, 82, 98n17
Five Dreamings (Michael Nelson Jagamara), 62
Foley, Fiona, 97n4
Fordham, Douglas, 99n25
Fowler Museum (Los Angeles), 9
framing, 14, 25, 31, 37, 43, 51, 61, 64, 69
French, Alison, 97n2, 99n26

gender, 34–35, 52, 61, 69, 83, 105n17. *See also* Men's Painting Room (Papunya)

geographies (sacred): depiction of, 12, 30, 51, 73; significance in Western Desert art, 41, 94; specific places, 14, 23, 31, 33, 39, 43–44, 48–50, 58–64. *See also* sacredness and protocols; Western Desert art
gift, politics of, 17
Gilchrist, Stephen, 3, 73, 89–90, 97–98n4, 101n5
Gillen, Francis, 49, 101n15, 103n5
Ginsburg, Faye, 10
Goanna Love Story (Shorty Lungkarta Tjungurrayi), 102n18
Graburn, Nelson, 97n1
Grey Art Gallery (New York), 9–10, 39
ground painting, 4–5, 23, 30, 33–34, 49, 74, 77–78, 97n2. *See also* body painting; sacredness and protocols; Western Desert art

Haasts Bluff (place), 15, 25
hair string, 32, 36, 42, 48, 50, 83, 93
Heidegger, Martin, 56
Herbert Johnson Museum (Ithaca), 9–10
Hermannsburg (place), 14–15, 75, 91, 102n1
Hogan, Pat, 13, 21–22, 30, 40, 99n24
Honey Ant Ancestors (Tim Leura Tjapaltjarri), 106n20
Honey Ant Ceremony (Clifford Possum Tjapaltjarri), 58, 75–77, 105nn14–15
Honey Ant Dreaming (mural at Papunya School), 7, 16
Honey Ant Dreaming (Tim Leura or Clifford Possum), 104n2
Honey Ant Dreaming (Version 3) (Clifford Possum Tjapaltjarri). See *Honey Ant Ceremony*

Iceman Dreaming (Wartuma Tjungurrayi). See *Wati G'wala*
Icons of the Desert (exhibition), 9–10, 39–40, 44, 48, 55, 67–69
Ilingawurrngawurrnga (place), 48
Ilpili (place), 23
Indigenous art: aesthetics of, 78–79; commercialization of, 6, 12, 14, 17–18, 97n1; as contemporary art, 1, 5, 15–18, 81, 87–89, 106n26; curation of, 3–4, 17, 81, 90, 97n2, 100n44; impact on art history and theory, 15–18, 22, 81, 86–89; modernism and, 15, 22–23, 59–60, 81, 100n46; non-Indigenous mediators and, 13, 86–89, 98n17, 98n23, 101n3; revelation and concealment in, 85; "traditional" versus "modern" in, 13–14; values in, 3, 18, 85, 88–89. *See also* sacredness and protocols; Western Desert art
Indigenous art centers, 13. *See also* Papunya School
Irriṯitja Kuwarri Tjungu (Past and Present Together) (Myers and Skerritt), 34–35, 94, 97n7, 100n43, 104n13

Jack-Hinton, Colin, 99n30
Jagamara, Michael Nelson, 62
Jensen, Michael, 8, 29, 55–58, 75, 101n1
John and Barbara Wilkerson Collection, 6, 9, 19, 21, 27, 30, 44, 67–68, 85, 98n13
Johnson, Vivien, 14, 22–23, 40, 44, 77, 98n11, 99n27, 102n5, 105n17
Jones, Jonathan, 4
Jorgensen, Darren, 97n2
Jung, Carl, 22

Kaapa, School of, 14–15, 55, 64, 77. *See also* Papunya Tula Pty. Ltd.; Tjampitjinpa, Kaapa Mbitjana; Western Desert art
Kalinpinypa (place; also spelled Kalipinynga), 23, 25, 55, 61, 64. See also *Water Dreaming at Kalinpinypa* (Johnny Warangkula Tjupurrula)
Kalkadoon, 4
Kean, John: agency of Papunya Tula artists, 13–15, 98n9; Clifford Possum, 106n22; collaboration between Papunya Tula painters, 51, 70, 104n7; Johnny Warangkula, 58–60; Kaapa Mbitjana, 103–4n5, 105n8; Namatjira, 105n15; painting and ceremony, 51, 59–60, 78–79; relationship to authors, 99n28
Kimber, Dick, 13, 30–31, 36, 60, 69, 101n3
Klingender, Tim, 9

Lampintjanya (place), 30–31, 33, 35
Land Rights, 15, 17. *See also* agency; displacement
Leura, Tim. *See* Tjapaltjarri, Tim Leura
Ligertwood Cliffs (place), 49
Long, Jeremy, 47
Lueyar, Ngawang Soepa, 102n5
Lungkarta, Shorty. *See* Tjungurrayi, Shorty Lungkarta
Luritja, 7, 23, 47, 91, 93

Malangi, David, 60
Man Corroboree (Mick Namarari Tjapaltjarri), 103n11
Man's Love Story (Clifford Possum Tjapaltjarri), 105n14, 106n24, 106n26
"map" painting, 15, 30, 62, 81
Marnpi (place), 47
Martin, Steve, 6
materials. *See* art materials
Mawurndjul, John, 59
McKenzie, Catriona, 98n15
McLean, Ian, 15–16, 102n5
Melville, Herman, 44
Men's Painting Room (Papunya), 10–11, 14, 56–57, 101n1, 105n14. *See also* Papunya School
methodologies. *See* multidisciplinarity
Mick and the Moon (film), 47
Mikanji (Kaapa Mbitjana Tjampitjinpa), 67
Mikanji (place), 62
Mikantji and Tywerle (Kaapa Mbitjana Tjampitjinpa), 103–4n5
Mitukatjirri (place), 47–48
Moby-Dick (Melville), 44
modernism, 1, 13–16, 18, 21–22, 98n23, 100n46. *See also* abstractionism; contemporary art
Moon Love Dreaming of Man and Woman—Medicine Story (Wartuma Tjungurrayi), 100n47
Morphy, Howard, 59, 97n2, 104n7
Mountford, Charles, 105n15
multidisciplinarity, 2–3, 18, 86–87. *See also* anthropology; art history and criticism; psychoanalysis; sociology
Mundine, Djon, 3, 87, 97n4
Munn, Nancy, 98n20
Murphy, Bernice, 81, 106n26
Muruntji (place), 35
Museum and Art Gallery of the Northern Territory (Darwin), 8–9, 16, 99n30
Museum of South Australia (Adelaide), 105n15
museums. *See* Australian Museum (Sydney); Fowler Museum (Los Angeles); Herbert Johnson Museum (Ithaca); Museum of South Australia (Adelaide); Yuendumu Men's Museum
Myers, Fred, 4–5, 10, 24, 85–89, 98n17, 99–100n42, 103n8. See also *Irritija Kuwarri Tjungu (Past and Present Together)*
Mystery Sand Mosaic (Shorty Lungkarta Tjungurrayi), 100n47

Namatjira, Albert, 14–15, 49, 75, 105n15
National Gallery of Australia (Canberra), 105n10
National Gallery of Victoria (Melbourne), 103n7
Neale, Margo, 3, 97
New York City (place), 6, 9, 11, 19, 22, 27, 68, 86
Ngalyipi (A Small Snake) (Kaapa Mbitjana Tjampitjinpa with Tim Leura Tjapaltjarri), 66–71, 73–75, 77–79, 82–83

O'Halloran, Alec, 102–3n1
Once Upon a Time in Papunya (Johnson), 14, 22–23

painting. *See* art materials; body painting; ground painting; "map" painting
Papunya (place), 1–20, 27, 58, 75, 85
Papunya: A Place Made after the Story (Bardon and Bardon), 8, 11–12, 22
Papunya Art and Craft Council, 8. *See also* Papunya Tula Artists Pty. Ltd
Papunya School, 7–8, 11, 16, 29, 57, 106n28. *See also* Men's Painting Room (Papunya)
Papunya Tula Artists Pty. Ltd., 8–9, 13, 101n3. *See also* Western Desert art

Papunya Tula: Art of the Western Desert (Bardon and Bardon), 11
Papunya Tula: Genesis and Genius (exhibition), 3–5, 14, 97
Parry, Terry, 43
Past and Present Together (Myers and Skerritt). See *Irritja Kuwarri Tjungu*
Paths of the Ancestors (Clifford Possum Tjapaltjarri), 62
Perkins, Hetti, 3–4, 17, 97n4
Phillipus, Long Jack. *See* Tjakamarra, Long Jack Phillipus
Phillips, Ruth B., 98n23
Pinchbeck, Cara, 4
Pintubi Revisit Yaru Yaru (film), 102n2, 103n2
Pintubi Revisit Yumari (film), 103n2
Pintupi: artists, 15, 30, 65; culture, 4, 16, 25, 36, 50; films, 103n2; geography, 7, 15; language, 7, 34–35, 40, 50, 69, 78, 91, 93–94; Luritja/Pintupi artists, 23, 47
Pintupi Revisit Mitukatjirri (film), 48
Pintupi Women's Bush Tucker Dreaming (John Scobie Tjapanangka), 100n47
Pitjantjatjarra, 16, 91
place. *See* displacement; geographies (sacred)
Place Made after the Story, A. See *Papunya: A Place Made after the Story* (Bardon and Bardon)
Possum, Clifford. *See* Tjapaltjarri, Clifford Possum
psychoanalysis, 21, 52
Pulpayella (Willy Tjungurrayi), 100n47

Radford, Ron, 106n26
Rain, Hail, and Lightning Dreaming at Waterhole (Version 1) (Wartuma Tjungurrayi), 100–101n5
Rain Dreaming Dance (Clifford Possum Tjapaltjarri), 77
Raising the Sky (Aspden), 81
Read, Herbert, 22
restricted viewing. *See* sacredness and protocols
Rey, Una, 11, 98n15
rock painting, 26, 97n2
Róheim, Géza, 52
Ryan, Allan J., 99n27
Ryan, Judith, 102n4, 103n7

sacredness and protocols: approaches to restriction, 63, 67, 103n4, 104n4; backlash against sharing sacred knowledge, 35–37, 49, 75–77, 103n2; ceremonial objects, 32–34, 36–37, 48–49, 52, 59, 75, 83, 103n4, 103n8; cultural protocols, 86–88; restricted knowledge, 1, 14, 23, 34–37, 94, 106–7n28; sacred designs, 51; unrestricted knowledge, 101n12, 102n18; veiling/doubling, 55–56, 75–77. *See also* doubling (aesthetics of); geographies (sacred); veiling (practice of); Western Desert art
Sandall, Roger, 47, 103n2
Sandhill Dancing (Version 1) (Kaapa Mbitjana Tjampitjinpa), 106n23
sand painting. *See* ground painting
Scholes, Luke, 16, 97, 99n28
secrecy. *See* sacredness and protocols
self-determination. *See* agency
Simpson, Audra, 86
Sims, Paddy Japaltjarri, 34
Skerritt, Henry, 34–35, 94. See also *Irritja Kuwarri Tjungu (Past and Present Together)*
Slade, Lisa, 75
Smith, Andrea, 86
Smith, Terry, 85–89, 99n30, 100n46, 106n25
sociology, 14
Spencer, Baldwin, 49, 101n15, 103n5
Spirit Dreaming through Napperby Country (Tim Leura Tjapaltjarri), 49, 81
Sprague, Quentin, 97n2
Stanner, W. E. H., 94
Stars, Rain, and Lightning at Night (Kingsley Tjungurrayi), 10, 20–23, 25–27, 41–42, 100–101n5
Stars at Night (Old Walter Tjampitjinpa), 100n2
Stephen, Ann, 99n30
Stockman, Billy, 69
Strehlow, T. G. H., 105n17

Stringfield, Anne, 6
Sutton, Peter, 99n27
Sweeney, Paul, 100n43

Tarawa, Charlie. *See* Tjungurrayi, Wartuma
Thomas, Nicholas, 87
Tingari Dreaming (Charlie Tjapangati), 81
Tjakamarra, Long Jack Phillipus, 1, 7, 16, 63–64, 97
Tjakamarra, Mick Wallankarri (Old Mick), 7, 14
Tjakamarra, Old Bert, 7
Tjampitjinpa, Kaapa Mbitjana, 7–8, 14–16, 25, 51, 55, 57–59, 62, 65–71, 73–75, 77–79, 82–83, 99n27, 103–4n5, 105n16, 106n23
Tjampitjinpa, Kenny Williams, 5
Tjampitjinpa, Old Walter, 56–58, 100n2
Tjangala, George, 31
Tjangala, Jeffrey James, 24
Tjangala, Left Hand Frank (aka Mungilnga), 31
Tjangala, Uta Uta, 15, 99–100n42
Tjapaltjarri, Benny, 47
Tjapaltjarri, Bill(y) Stockman, 7
Tjapaltjarri, Clifford Possum: as Anmatyerr artist, 15, 65; growth and influences, 25, 58, 75, 77, 100n47, 106n26; Honey Ant Dreaming, 104n2, 106n24; "map" paintings, 62; reproductions of paintings by, 76; sacred knowledge and, 59, 81, 105n14; Snake Dreaming, 69–70, 79, 106n22. See also *Honey Ant Ceremony*; *Two Snakes at Alinitti; Untitled (Snake Dreaming)*; *Warlugulong*; *Women's Dreaming about Bush Tucker, Yarlga*
Tjapaltjarri, Mick Namarari, 8, 15, 35, 46–53, 102–3n1. See also *Man Corroboree*
Tjapaltjarri, Tim Leura, 49–51, 59, 62, 65–70, 75, 77–78, 81, 104n2, 106n20. See also *Ngalyipi (A Small Snake)*
Tjapaltjarri, Warlimpirrnga, 5
Tjapanangka, Allen, 43
Tjapanangka, John Scobie, 100n47
Tjapangati, Charlie, 5, 81
Tjapangati, Timmy Payungka, 8, 56–57
Tjaruru, Charlie. *See* Tjungurrayi, Wartuma
Tjitururrnga (place), 39–40, 43
Tjukurrtjanu, 94
Tjungunutja, from having come together (exhibition), 16
Tjungurrayi, Kingsley, 10, 20–23, 25–27, 41–42, 64, 100–101n5
Tjungurrayi, Shorty Lungkarta, 8, 10, 15, 28–37, 41, 48, 58, 74, 100n47, 101n4. See also *Goanna Love Story*
Tjungurrayi, Wartuma (Charlie Tarawa/Tjaruru), 15, 31, 38–45, 52, 91, 99–100n42, 100n47, 100–101n5, 102n5
Tjungurrayi, Willy, 100n47
Tjungurrayi, Yala Yala Gibbs, 8, 56
Tjupurrula, Bobby West, 5, 16
Tjupurrula, Johnny Warangkula, 8–9, 15, 23, 30, 53–65, 67, 70, 75
Tjupurrula, Turkey Tolson, 48, 65
translation, 11–12, 18, 30, 34, 40, 52, 69, 85–86, 94
Trial, The (Wartuma Tjungurrayi), 31, 38–45
Two Snakes at Alinitti (Clifford Possum Tjapaltjarri), 79, 106nn21–22

Ulay, 102n5
Untitled (Kaapa Mbitjana Tjampitjinpa), 105n16
Untitled (Snake Dreaming) (Clifford Possum Tjapaltjarri), 70, 72–73

veiling (practice of), 55–56, 58–60, 63–64, 70. *See also* sacredness and protocols; Western Desert art
Vorano, Norman, 98n23

Warangkula, Johnny. *See* Tjupurrula, Johnny Warangkula
Warlpiri, 7, 16, 34, 83, 91, 104n4, 104n6
Warlugulong (Clifford Possum Tjapaltjarri), 81–82
Warlukurlangu Artists, 101n10
Water Dreaming (Kingsley Tjungurrayi), 100n5
Water Dreaming at Kalinpinypa (Johnny Warangkula Tjupurrula), 9, 23, 30, 54–65, 75

Wati G'wala (Iceman Dreaming) (Wartuma Tjungurrayi), 44
weaving, 82–83
Weislogel, Andrew, 9
Western Desert art: abstraction in, 18, 21–23, 59, 79, 105n14; artist compensation and, 15, 17, 99–100n42; (artistic) agency and, 11–18, 86, 88–90, 98n9; children and, 34–36, 102n18; commercial market for, 9, 13–14, 98n11; European imagery and, 7, 78; as "gifts," 2, 17–18; iconography of, 12, 22–23, 35, 55–56; Indigenous/non-Indigenous relations and, 2–7, 11–18, 25, 30, 40, 44–45, 86–89, 101n3, 102n5; influence on contemporary art, 1, 5, 15–19, 21–23, 59, 79, 81, 87–88, 102n5, 105n14, 106n26; modernism and, 1, 13–16, 18, 21–22, 98n23, 100n46; naming and, 12, 23, 26, 35, 68, 102n5; perspective in, 12, 23, 30, 48, 51, 74; relation to ceremony, 14, 16, 32, 36–37, 42, 51, 59, 63–64, 75–79; in relation to Western art-culture system, 2, 25, 30, 59, 81, 85, 97n1; "sacred geographies" of, 12, 31, 33, 39, 43–44, 48–50, 60–64; significance of place in, 14, 23, 30, 41, 58–63, 73, 94; transcultural translation in, 11–12, 18, 30, 34, 40, 52, 69, 85–86. *See also* art materials; body painting; Central Australian movement; doubling (aesthetics of); framing; ground painting; Indigenous art; Kaapa, School of; Papunya (place); veiling (practice of); women artists; *individual artists*
Wilkerson Collection. *See* John and Barbara Wilkerson Collection
Williams, Daphne, 13, 44
Winparrku Serpents, The (Kaapa Mbitjana Tjampitjinpa), 70–71
women artists, 4, 62, 86
Women's Dreaming about Bush Tucker, Yarlga (Clifford Possum Tjapaltjarri), 79–80

Yamatji, 3, 89
Yaru Yaru (place), 48
Yuendumu (place), 13, 56, 69, 77, 104n4
Yuendumu Men's Museum, 104n4
Yumari (place), 48